Essex

A Hidden Aviation History

PAUL BINGLEY AND RICHARD E. FLAGG

AMBERLEY

Acknowledgements

The authors wish to thank the following for their invaluable help and assistance: Tony Hibberd and Paul Cannon.

First published 2020

Amberley Publishing
The Hill, Stroud,
Gloucestershire, GL5 4EP

www.amberley-books.com

ISBN 978 1 4456 9481 8 (print)
ISBN 978 1 4456 9482 5 (ebook)

British Library Cataloguing in Publication Data.
A catalogue record for this book is available from the British Library.

Typeset in 10pt on 13pt Celeste.
Typesetting by Aura Technology and Software Services, India.
Printed in the UK.

Contents

Preface

'I watched the Battle of Britain from my back garden'. So said Ernie Merton in 2012.

Ernie had been a schoolboy during the Second World War. After marvelling at Spitfires and Messerschmitts tangling over his Essex home during the summer of 1940, his ears then became finely tuned to the sound of American Flying Fortresses as they lumbered overhead in 1943. Most days, he would cycle to his nearest airfield to watch them return ('very low and with bits falling off them'). Almost seventy years on, Ernie could still clearly picture them.

Stories like Ernie's are those we often hear, yet we barely see Essex as an aerial battleground or aviation hotbed. However, for over a century it has been.

Located beneath the shortest flight path between north-west Europe and London, Essex was overflown by many thousands of military aircraft during both world wars. These days, sleek Boeings and Airbuses shuttle people of every nationality across its 350-mile-long coastline. Few are able to distinguish the county or its aviation heritage below, while on the ground it's even harder to see. Yet the signs are all there.

Erected on village greens, placed in fields or fixed to the walls of churches, these markers represent a significant contribution to British aviation. They point to groundbreaking events, frequent tragedies and scores of sacrifices.

This book looks back at Essex's key aerial moments while providing a guide to its many scattered memorials. We hope it inspires the reader to take off and explore a rich aviation heritage that is now largely hidden from view.

Ernie Merton's Spitfires and Fortresses may have long since flown, but their stories have been set in stone. One just needs to know where to look.

Paul Bingley & Richard E. Flagg

Chapter One

Flight and Fight

Fifteen centuries after Chinese warriors first sent small flame-filled lanterns into the air to summon help during battle, two French brothers took the idea to another level.

Tethering an object to the ground in Ardèche, France, Joseph-Michel and Jacques-Étienne Montgolfier lit a small fire. Hot air then filled its body, which ascended into the sky. For a brief ten-minute period in 1783, the Montgolfier brothers' unmanned balloon became the catalyst for modern aviation.

Few people in Essex were aware of this groundbreaking event, but things changed when fellow Frenchman and 'aeronaut' Jean-Pierre Blanchard arrived in England a year later.

Obsessed with the idea of flying, Blanchard was seeking financial backing for his own aerial ambition – to fly across the English Channel. By early 1785, he had succeeded

An artist's impression of French balloon pioneer Jean-Pierre Blanchard. Blanchard made the first flight across the English Channel in 1785, before making the first recorded landing in Essex. (Authors' Collection)

in making the first successful balloon flight from England to France. Six months later, Blanchard brought the idea of aviation to the county of Essex.

Lifting off from Chelsea, he drifted across London before landing 25 miles away on Langdon Hills, near Basildon. According to one local man who witnessed the event, Blanchard then 'pac'd it up in a post-chaise and went to London'.

Remarkably, just two weeks later another balloon landed in a field near Fambridge. Jean-Pierre Blanchard was not at the controls this time, but Major John Money – a member of the British 'Balloon Club'. Essex had inadvertently become one of Britain's earliest 'landing grounds'.

The first ascent by an Essex man took place nearly fifty years later when scientist and astronomer George Nash of Elsenham Hall, near Bishop's Stortford, rose to a height of 19,000 feet (5,800 metres) to test his new barometer. Six days later, a second attempt saw Nash and British 'aeronaut' Charles Green achieve a record ascent of 27,146 feet (8,300 metres) – although both men suffered 'head swellings and bleedings from the eyes and ears' in the process.

Over the next seventy years, Essex men strove to fly by any means. George Faux began experimenting with aeronautics by jumping from his roof in Chigwell Row and employing the use of 'flapping wings'. Threats of prosecution quickly ended his airborne exploits.

Another pioneering British 'aeronaut', Joseph Simmons, was then commissioned by Sir Claude Champion de Crespigny of Champion Lodge, Ulting, to fly him across the North Sea. In June 1882 both men landed in Arras, France, after a flight of '12 minutes'. This was followed two months later by another crossing to Flushing in Belgium. Both flights had taken off from the same field in Maldon. Five years later, though, the intrepid Simmons was killed in an accident on de Crespigny's estate while preparing for a long-distance flight to Vienna. Aviation was fast becoming a dangerous affair.

The American Wright brothers safely wrote themselves into the history books after making the first powered, heavier-than-air human flight on 17 December 1903. Three months earlier, however, British engineer and aerodynamicist Horatio Phillips had demonstrated his new 'multi-plane' in Essex. Trialling the engine-driven machine on St Lawrence Hill near Southminster, Phillips claimed to have reached a height of 3 feet (1 metre) over a distance of 30 yards (28 metres). Although his boast was corroborated by a witness, Phillips's 'achievement' was never recognised.

Noel Pemberton Billing was an Englishman who did go on to achieve great aviation fame. Having fought during the Second Boer War, Billing was then invalided back to England, where he developed a keen interest in aviation. In 1908 he moved to Burnham-on-Crouch, where he started work on the construction of an experimental flying machine. He found a new site for its testing on flat marshland at South Fambridge, which he soon called the 'Colony of British Aerocraft'. His 'colony' was briefly used by several individuals to construct and test their own machines, including one financed by Frederick Handley Page, who visited Fambridge in 1909. However, the boggy Essex ground proved unsuitable for the testing of 'aerocraft' and Billing was forced to relocate to Southampton. Here, he established Supermarine – a company that would enjoy great success in the Schneider seaplane races before going on to design the country's most famous fighter, the Spitfire.

Just as Billing was struggling to establish Britain's first 'aerodrome', another British aviation pioneer was busy constructing his triplane 30 miles away on Walthamstow Marshes – then in the county of Essex.

Above left: Noel Pemberton Billing was born in 1881. After serving during the Second Boer War, he established Britain's earliest aerodrome at Fambridge before going on to help establish Supermarine in 1913. (Authors' Collection)

Above right: One of two plaques fixed to a railway arch at Walthamstow Marshes, this commemorates Alliot Verdon Roe's first successful flight in an 'all-British aeroplane powered by a British engine'. (Authors' Collection)

Alliot Verdon Roe had previously discovered two derelict railway arches that opened out onto an expanse of grassland. In June 1909, he rolled out his 'Roe 1' triplane and bounced it into the air for a series of 50-foot (16-metre) jumps, which earned him the nickname 'The Hopper'. Roe's tenacity saw him become the first Briton to 'fly' an all-British aeroplane powered by a British engine. Like Handley Page, who had already established Handley Page Ltd 'for the business of manufacturer in aeroplanes, hydroplanes, airships, balloons, aeronautical apparatus and machines' at Creekmouth, Barking, Alliot Verdon Roe's name would become synonymous with British military aviation. His company, Avro, would eventually design and build the country's legendary heavy bomber, the Lancaster. Thus these two great British aircraft manufacturers, Avro and Handley Page, could be said to have had their origins in Essex.

The development of flying machines soon led to a growth in aviation support. Everard Calthrop of Loughton was a prominent railway engineer and inventor. He was also a close friend of Charles Rolls – another pioneering British aviator and co-founder of Rolls-Royce. On 12 July 1910, Calthrop accompanied Rolls to Bournemouth for an aviation meeting. During Rolls's flying display, however, his aircraft snapped in two, sending the machine plummeting out of control. He became the first Briton to be killed in an aeronautical accident using a powered aircraft. Calthrop believed that parachutes could be used to save aviators in the event of such catastrophes. Three years later, he patented his first design.

Above: The Handley Page works at Creekmouth, Barking, pictured around 1909. The company would later go on to produce the famous Halifax bomber, as well as civil airliners. (Authors' Collection)

Left: Everard Calthrop's 'Guardian Angel' parachute undergoes testing. Calthrop lived at Goldings, Loughton, where a blue plaque now recognises his achievements as an engineer and parachute pioneer. (Authors' Collection)

On 26 June 1912, Claude Grahame-White – Britain's 'matinee idol of the air' – married New York heiress Dorothy Chadwell Taylor in a service at St Mary's Church, Widford, near Chelmsford. A reception then took place at nearby Hylands Park, where two biplanes performed a flying display. Grahame-White was one of the first Britons to qualify as a pilot and was the country's most celebrated aviator. He went on to establish Hendon Aerodrome, which became the location for another first in British aviation.

In 1914, a Grahame-White Type X Charabanc five-seater biplane took to the sky over Hendon carrying a single passenger – William Newell. He was onboard to make the very first parachute descent from an aeroplane. The parachute tested by Newell was Everard Calthrop's so-called 'Guardian Angel'. Newell's gallant (and successful) attempt meant that aviators would have some hope of surviving an accident.

First Sea Lord Winston Churchill had almost required the use of a 'Guardian Angel' just two weeks before. During an inspection of air stations along the East Anglian coast, his Short S.74 seaplane developed an engine problem en route to Felixstowe.

Britain's 'matinee idol of the air', Claude Grahame-White, poses with his wife, Dorothy Taylor, on a Henry Farman 1909 biplane. Grahame-White would go on to establish Hendon Aerodrome. (Authors' Collection)

A stone monolith in Clacton still commemorates Winston Churchill's forced landing close to the town's pier in April 1914. (Richard E. Flagg)

Churchill's pilot had no option but to force-land close to Clacton Pier, off the town's West Beach. Unperturbed, Churchill walked the short distance to the Royal Hotel, where he remained until a replacement seaplane was sent to collect him.

Churchill's unscheduled stop in Clacton came two months before events in Sarajevo sparked what would become the First World War. Several days after Archduke Franz Ferdinand's assassination, Britain's Royal Naval Air Service (RNAS) was given the task of home defence, while much of the Royal Flying Corps (RFC) was despatched to France. Several weeks later, Austria-Hungary's shelling of the Serbian capital, Belgrade, saw the arrival of the first military aircraft to be based in Essex.

The RNAS quickly formed a 'sub-station' of Kent's RNAS Grain on an 800-yard section of Clacton's West Beach, close to where Churchill had landed four months earlier. Three S.74 seaplanes – the same type that had unintentionally delivered Churchill to Essex – then arrived to begin their operational duties.

Following the German invasion of Belgium two days later, Britain declared war on Germany. The newly invoked Defence of the Realm Act then saw an aerial defence system of gun batteries, searchlights and observers placed around London, while a total blackout was also imposed. The government then began surveying land and buildings beyond the capital's suburbs to accommodate new aeroplane 'landing grounds'.

Sixty acres of farmland were promptly purchased from a local farmer near Hainault and handed to the RNAS. By October 1914, RNAS Hainault Farm – named for the farm itself – became a 'day landing ground'. At the same time, twenty-two acres of farmland close to Writtle were levelled and prepared to provide a temporary RNAS landing ground, while more farmland was acquired at Rochford, Chingford, Burnham-on-Crouch and Widford. The first two were initially classified as 'home defence' stations for the RNAS, while the smaller Burnham-on-Crouch and Widford landing grounds soon became two 'branch stations'. Their openings proved timely.

On 19 January 1915, the first German Zeppelin airship slipped over England. Capable of travelling at 85 miles per hour, the Zeppelins would eventually instil 'a special kind of fear' in the British people. The Essex public heard the Zeppelin 'roar' for the first time on 21 February, when a solitary airship crossed over the coast at Clacton before heading towards Braintree, where two bombs were dropped. The remainder of the Zeppelin's load was then discharged over both Coggeshall and Colchester. The targets for the airship that night were thought to be the Marconi wireless masts at Chelmsford. Fortunately, both the masts and Essex's inhabitants survived.

Nuisance raids followed through April before Zeppelin LZ.38 arrived over Southend-on-Sea on the night of 9 May 1915. This 536-foot-long airship – the first to be built and assigned to the Imperial Germany Army – dropped over 100 bombs on the Essex town, making it the heaviest bombing raid on Britain so far. The Germans also delivered a chilling 'calling card': 'You English! We have come and will come again. Kill or cure. German!'

Unfortunately, there was no cure for Agnes Whitwell of Prittlewell. She was killed in the raid, which came just two days after the controversial sinking of the British ocean liner RMS *Lusitania*. The combination of the two events led to an outbreak of anti-German sentiment, culminating in violent attacks on businesses thought to be German-owned. Only after soldiers were called in was order finally restored.

Britain's first heavy bombing raid was followed by the first attack on London. On 31 May, LZ.38 returned to England, dropping 1,400 kg (3,000 lb) of bombs on East London,

Taken at the end of the First World War, Hainault Farm's airmen are pictured outside a repair hangar inscribed with the German word, *Kadaververwertungsanstalt* – Corpse Factory. (JMB/GSL Collection)

'Super Zeppelin' L33, which eventually crashed at Little Wigborough, undergoes a test flight in Germany. By August 1918, the Zeppelin raids had killed more than 500 British civilians. (Authors' Collection)

which killed seven people. The Zeppelin was sighted by an RNAS Blériot Parasol pilot flying from Rochford, but engine failure forced his aircraft to land. Reporting restrictions were then introduced by the British government to suppress a growing public anxiety.

To hinder the Zeppelins' unchecked movements over Essex, the spread of RNAS landing grounds gathered speed. In August 1915, Gardener's Farm, 3 miles north-east of Maldon, saw the appearance of a pilot, who was immediately offered 'bed and breakfast' at its farmhouse. Shortly afterwards, five fields measuring some 77 acres were purchased from the farmer and his near neighbour. Eventually named Goldhanger, it became a flight station that would remain in operation until March 1919.

At Sutton's Farm near Hornchurch, around 105 acres of land had also been purchased. Within weeks, two portable aircraft hangars and several tents were erected. The RFC's

The Gardeners Farm Shop, located on Goldhanger's former flight station, commemorates the airfield's First World War activities with this plaque, unveiled by a local history group in 2015. (Richard E. Flagg)

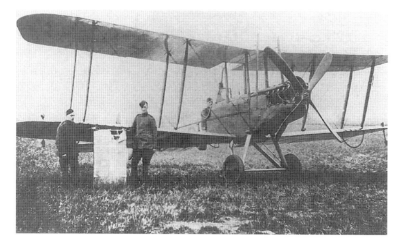

Lieutenant William Leefe Robinson of No. 39 Squadron in his Royal Aircraft Factory B.E.2c at Sutton's Farm. The ground crew hold a section of his upper wing, which he inadvertently shot off. (Authors' Collection)

No. 23 Squadron arrived shortly afterwards with its Royal Aircraft Factory B.E.2s. A few days later, on 13 October, the squadron intercepted its first Zeppelin.

At 9:05 p.m., eighteen-year-old Second Lieutenant Jack Slessor began a 45-minute climb to reach his assigned patrol altitude of 10,000 feet (3,000 metres). At the same time, Zeppelin L.15 was returning across London having bombed Charing Cross.

One of five Zeppelins operating over England, L.15 had taken part in the deadliest raid on Britain, killing seventy-one people and injuring 128. As it overflew Romford, the Zeppelin was lit by searchlights. Slessor caught sight of it, but as he prepared to attack, the airship slipped into a cloudbank and disappeared. A frustrated Slessor returned to Sutton's Farm, where he misjudged his landing and buckled his aeroplane's undercarriage. Despite this, 'Jack' went on to become Sir John Slessor, Marshal of the Royal Air Force.

By February 1916 – and with the RNAS failing to prevent the Zeppelin raids – the RFC was handed responsibility for Britain's home defence. With many of its operational squadrons still in France, it fell to the RFC's training units to supply the necessary aeroplanes. One of those was No. 19 Reserve Aeroplane Squadron, which eventually became No. 39 (Home Defence) Squadron, based at Sutton's Farm.

On 31 March, New Zealander Alfred de Bathe Brandon of No. 19 Reserve Aeroplane Squadron, flying his B.E.2 fighter, spotted Zeppelin L.15 (previously sighted by Jack Slessor in October 1915) overflying the Thames Estuary. The airship had also been chased across Orsett by several pilots from Hainault Farm. L.15 was subsequently attacked and damaged by gun batteries along the Thames before Brandon managed to drop several explosive darts onto it. The airship crashed down in the sea, 15 miles from Margate – the first Zeppelin to be brought down while over British territory. Brandon was duly awarded the Military Cross for his actions.

Over the next few months more landing grounds were opened across Essex. Fairlop – located less than half a mile from Hainault Farm – was joined by Beaumont, East Hanningfield (one of the highest points in Essex), Horndon-on-the-Hill, Mountnessing, North Benfleet, North Ockendon and Sible Hedingham. By the end of 1916, sixteen new aerodromes had been established in the county – including Stow Maries, which figures prominently in Essex's aviation heritage today.

12

Compulsorily purchased from two farmers near South Woodham Ferrers in August 1916, Stow Maries covered some 118 acres and was immediately equipped with four aeroplane sheds and several support buildings. Although it would be eight months before the first operational sorties were flown, a section of No. 37 (Home Defence) Squadron arrived with its Royal Aircraft Factory B.E.2s a month later.

North Weald Bassett – another Essex landing ground that would go on to have a long and distinguished history – was also established in August. Within days of its opening, a pilot of No. 39 (Home Defence) Squadron chased a Zeppelin over Essex before running short of fuel. Fortunately, he managed to make an emergency landing at the newly opened Burnham-on-Crouch landing ground.

Four weeks later, fourteen Zeppelins and two Schütte-Lanz airships carried out raids on London and the Midlands. One of the latter – S.L.11, which had first flown a month earlier – dropped its heavy payload over St Albans before making an escape. Lieutenant William Leefe Robinson of No. 39 Squadron had already taken off in his B.E.2 from Sutton's

Aircraft of the Royal Naval Air Service (RNAS) overfly Fairlop during the First World War. A training centre for the RNAS, more men died learning to fly here than in combat with Zeppelins. (Authors' Collection)

An artist's impression of Stow Maries showing its maintenance and storage buildings, as well as its regimental buildings consisting of accommodation blocks and a sizeable mess hall. (Stow Maries Great War Aerodrome)

One half of an original First World War Twin Shed (hangar) that was originally sited at North Weald Aerodrome. Pictured at Moreton in 2009, its last use was as a garage/workshop. Despite efforts to save and relocate it to Stow Maries, it was demolished in 2010. (Richard E. Flagg)

Farm when he spotted the airship caught in searchlights. Using incendiary ammunition, he attacked three times before S.L.11 finally burst into flames and crashed near Cuffley, Hertfordshire. Hauptmann Wilhelm Schramm and his crew of fifteen were killed, their airship becoming the first to be shot down over the British mainland. As a result, William Leefe Robinson was hailed as a national hero. He was promptly awarded the Victoria Cross and given £4,200 in public money.

Three weeks later, on 23 September 1916, no less than twelve Zeppelins were despatched to carry out attacks on England. Among the flotilla were four R-class models – 650-foot-long 'Super Zeppelins', capable of carrying a 5-ton bomb load. The four steered varying courses for London, while the RFC's pilots scurried to find them.

Kapitän Leutnant Werner Petersen was in command of L.32, which had crossed the coast at Dungeness before heading north. Intense ground fire from gun batteries soon forced him to adjust his course for Aveley and Hornchurch, where he dropped his bombs – four of which landed in and around Sutton's Farm landing ground. It was from here that several B.E.2s had already taken off, including that of Second Lieutenant Frederick Sowrey. Spotting the Zeppelin pinpointed by searchlights, Sowrey quickly closed in and opened fire. After two failed attempts, he swapped his machine gun's drum for incendiary bullets. A concentrated burst then saw L.32 catch fire and crash at Snail's Hall Farm, Great Burstead, killing all twenty-two crew members. Sowrey was subsequently awarded the Distinguished Service Order and promoted to captain, before being made commanding officer of Goldhanger Flight Station.

Zeppelin L.33 had also taken part in the raid. By 11 p.m. it was flying at 13,000 feet (3,962 metres) over London. Amid heavy groundfire, its captain, Alois Böcker, dropped his bombs on Bromley-by-Bow. Shortly afterwards, L.33 was struck by anti-aircraft fire. With a

Right: Captain William Leefe Robinson VC was the first RFC pilot to shoot down a Zeppelin. A huge public reaction saw money, letters and telegrams pour in, making Leefe Robinson a wealthy man. (Authors' Collection)

Below: British military officers inspect the twisted remains of 'Super Zeppelin' L32, which crashed at Snails Hall Farm, Great Burstead, on 23 September 1916, after being downed by Second Lieutenant Frederick Sowrey. (Authors' Collection)

damaged gas holding cell, main ring and bracing cable, his airship began venting hydrogen and lost altitude. Despite frantic attempts by the crew to jettison loose items and fuel, L.33 was soon descending at 800 feet (245 metres) per minute.

Lieutenant Alfred de Bathe Brandon of No. 39 Squadron (who had previously brought L.15 down in the sea in March) was patrolling in his B.E.2 when he caught sight of L.33 and intercepted it near Kelvedon Hatch. Fighting not only the Zeppelin but his own aircraft (Brandon's automatic petrol pump immediately failed and one of his Lewis guns had dropped from its mounting), he managed to empty a full drum of mixed bullets into L.33. After attacking for 20 minutes, he exhausted his supply of ammunition and watched the Zeppelin slip away. Brandon flew back to Hainault Farm with nothing to show for his efforts.

Alois Böcker continued steering the Zeppelin towards the North Sea, but damage from the attacks had left L.33 flying at a nose-high attitude. Descending awkwardly over Witham, Maldon and Tolleshunt Major, the crew's desperate cries could be heard by those on the ground. Finally, at 1.20 a.m., L.33 struck Essex soil at Copt Hall Lane, Little Wigborough, just 20 yards from a row of cottages. Incredibly, L.33 remained virtually intact. The crew of twenty-two had also escaped largely unscathed. Aware that the British would benefit from a detailed inspection of the wreckage, Böcker elected to set fire to the Zeppelin. Before doing so, however, he knocked on the door of the nearby cottages to warn the residents. Cowering inside, their doors remained firmly locked.

A short while later, Special Constable Edgar Nicholas in nearby Peldon was awoken by an explosion. Hastening to the scene of the blast on his bicycle, he approached a group of men walking towards him:

> I at once dismounted and addressing the leader, asked: 'Is it a Zeppelin down?' He said, 'How many miles is it to Colchester?' I replied, 'About six'. He replied, 'Thank you'. I at once recognised a foreign accent and from their clothing and conversation knew they were Germans. I received no answer to my question.

Nicholas followed the crew to Peldon Post Office, where Police Constable Charles Smith was on hand to formally arrest them. They were then escorted to Mersea Strood, where they were handed over to the British Army. Charles Smith was duly promoted to the rank of sergeant and given the nickname 'Zepp' by locals.

The pilots of No. 39 Squadron stepped up their battle with the Zeppelins. A week after the loss of L.32 and L.33, another R-Class model – L.31 (a veteran of six attacks on England) –

The Lewis family, residents of New Hall Cottages, Copt Hall Lane, Little Wigborough, pose in front of their home with the wreckage of 'Super Zeppelin' L33 in the background. (Authors' Collection)

16

found itself on the receiving end of Lieutenant Wulstan Tempest's B.E.2, which had taken off from North Weald Bassett. The Zeppelin, captained by Germany's leading airship commander of the time, Heinrich Mathy, had dropped most of its bombs over Cheshunt, Hertfordshire. Tempest then spotted it some way in the distance. Although fuel pump problems hampered his pursuit, he was able to catch the Zeppelin, firing two bursts of incendiary bullets from behind and below. Tempest later described how he saw a red glow burst from inside the Zeppelin, making it appear 'like an enormous Chinese lantern'. Moments later, fire spewed from its bow and the airship went down in flames over Potters Bar. Mathy and his entire crew were killed as they jumped from the burning Zeppelin.

The loss of Mathy was a huge blow for the Germans. For Wulstan Tempest, however, the attack had left him exhausted. Landing back at North Weald Bassett, he crashed his aircraft, cracking his head against the butt of his machine gun. To add insult to injury, he was forced to pay a shilling the next day to view the wreckage of L.31 along with hundreds of others.

By March 1917, the government declared that just seventy-one RFC pilots had been engaged in home defence duties. Described as a 'thin line of young men with their flimsy machines bravely and valiantly battling in the night skies against the monstrous Zepps', Tempest and his fellow pilots had ensured that L.31 was the very last Zeppelin to reach London. Nevertheless, the Germans had produced a new type of bomber that would present a very different challenge to the RFC pilots.

The Gotha G.IV was a 40-foot-long twin 'pusher' biplane that had been delivered to the German Army High Command in March 1917. On 25 May of that year, twenty-three Gothas commenced a series of raids on targets in England. Although two were forced to turn back with mechanical problems, twenty-one others flew on during Operation Türkenkreuz (Turk's Cross), an attempt to demoralise the British public.

Crossing the Essex coast between the rivers Crouch and Blackwater, the Gothas headed for London. Described by some as 'high white machines making a loud noise', they were quickly targeted by a mobile gun battery at Burnham-on-Crouch. Twenty RFC fighters then took off from several Essex aerodromes to intercept them. Two pilots from

A German Gotha bomber, pictured with a gunner and pilot (the dorsal gunner is not shown). Principally used as night bombers, Gothas were first used against Britain during Operation Türkenkreuz in May 1917. (Authors' Collection)

No. 37 Squadron found their B.E.12s to be 'completely unsuitable for chasing such hostile aircraft', having taken half an hour to reach 15,000 feet (4,500 metres). By this time, the Gothas had flown 35 miles away. Finding London cloud-covered, the German bombers then turned towards their secondary target at Folkestone, Kent. Unleashing their bombs, they caused extensive damage to an army barracks, which killed eighteen soldiers. A further seventy-seven civilians also lost their lives, while 195 others were injured. Eleven days later, twenty Gothas returned to England. Several bombs were dropped on Shoeburyness and Great Wakering, but their target (London) was once again spared by bad weather. The next week, however, fourteen bombers got their chance to strike the capital.

Over a hundred bombs were dropped, many of which landed within a mile of Liverpool Street station. A school in Poplar was also destroyed, killing eighteen children. What became known as 'Black Wednesday' saw a total of 162 people lose their lives to the Gotha bombers. A further 426 were injured. *The Times* newspaper was unequivocal in its response, claiming the raid 'slew women and children as well as men... and increased the utter and most universal detestation with which the Hun is held by the people of this country'.

Although the RFC pilots were having little success in preventing the Gotha raids, just three days later the fifth and final Zeppelin to be brought down over England, Zeppelin L.48, was shot down over the North Sea near Leiston, Norfolk, by Second Lieutenant Loudon Watkins of Goldhanger's No. 37 Squadron.

Nevertheless, the Gothas continued their onslaught, attacking Harwich, Felixstowe and London over a three-day period in July 1917. Although three bombers were brought down over the Thames Estuary and in the North Sea by a combination of RFC and RNAS fighters, another seventy-four people were killed in the raids.

One RNAS pilot who had his own pioneering feats to attend to was Squadron Commander Edwin Dunning. Born in South Africa, Dunning's family lived at Jacques Hall, Bradfield. Awarded a Distinguished Service Cross in March 1916 for 'exceptionally good work as a seaplane flyer', Dunning was also mentioned in despatches for his service at Gallipoli. On 8 August 1917, Dunning duly wrote himself into the history books after landing a Sopwith Pup on the deck of HMS *Furious* in Scapa Flow, becoming the first person to land an aeroplane on a moving ship at sea.

Not content with one successful attempt, Dunning tried to repeat the exploit five days later. During his first landing, a gust of wind caught the aircraft, damaging its elevator. Switching to a replacement Pup, he tried again. Approaching the ship, Dunning quickly realised that he was too far forward and waved the deck crew away. As he opened the throttle to gain height, his engine lost power and the aircraft stalled. The Pup slammed onto the deck and careered over the side of the ship. Moments later, HMS *Furious* sailed over the aircraft. It was subsequently found that Dunning had been knocked unconscious and drowned. He was later buried in St Lawrence's Church, Bradfield, where part of his memorial inscription reads:

The Admiralty wish you to know what great service he performed for the Navy. It was in fact a demonstration of landing an aeroplane on the deck of a Man-of-War while the latter was underway. This had never been done before; and the data obtained was of the utmost value. It will make aeroplanes indispensable to a fleet; & possibly revolutionise Naval Warfare.

A memorial to Edwin Harris Dunning in St Lawrence's Church, Bradfield, Essex, commemorates his achievement as the first airman to land an aircraft on a moving ship at sea in August 1917. (Richard E. Flagg)

Five days after Dunning's death, German Gothas carried out what would be their last daylight attack on England. On 12 August 1917, thirty-four bombs were dropped in and around Southend-on-Sea, causing thirty-three fatalities. Most of those affected were day-trippers from an armaments factory in Braintree.

It would be a further four months before the first German aeroplane was brought down over Britain at night. Captain Gilbert W. M. Green of No. 44 (Home Defence) Squadron, flying his Sopwith Camel night fighter from Hainault Farm, first tried unsuccessfully to attack a Gotha over Essex. Returning to Hainault Farm to refuel, he eventually intercepted another over Kent. A sustained attack saw it crash in the sea off Folkestone.

On 28 January 1918, No. 44 Squadron again got the measure of the German Gothas. Two pilots flying from Hainault Farm – Captain G. H. Hackwell and Lieutenant Charles C. Banks – both attacked the same bomber over Wickford, successfully bringing it down near the town with the loss of its three crewmen. It was the first Gotha to be brought down over British soil. The crew was later buried with full military honours at St Margaret's Church in Downham, before being reinterred at the German Military Cemetery at Cannock Chase, Staffordshire.

Contending with the Gothas was one thing, but the Germans had also begun to deploy another type of heavy bomber to Britain. The Zeppelin-Staaken R.VI was a four-engine biplane capable of carrying up to 2,000 kg (4,400 lb) of bombs. Named Riesenflugzeug ('giant aeroplane'), the bomber had begun raiding London on 28 September 1917 by following the course of the River Thames.

On 17 February 1918, one 'Giant' found its way across London, where it bombed St Pancras station. The raid cost the lives of twenty-one people, with thirty-two injured. Some seventy home defence fighters were involved in trying to intercept the bomber, including the B.E.12 of eighteen-year-old Sydney Armstrong, flying from Goldhanger. Armstrong managed to attack the aircraft but suffered engine damage in the process. His fighter came down in a field between Goldhanger and Tolleshunt Major, killing him instantly. Lieutenant Armstrong was buried in St Peter's Church, Goldhanger.

The race to intercept the German bombers (and train pilots to do so) was becoming deadlier. Just nine days later, Sydney Armstrong's replacement, Second Lieutenant Frederick

The scale of the Zeppelin-Staaken R.VI 'Giant' can clearly be seen in this aerial image. Its wingspan of 42.2 metres (138 feet) almost equalled that of the Second World War Boeing B-29 Superfortress. (Authors' Collection)

Crowley, was killed in a flying accident when his Sopwith Camel crashed near the village of Goldhanger. Like Armstrong, he was buried in the grounds of St Peter's Church.

Even those with experience were not immune to accidents. Just nine days later, Essex-born Gallipoli veteran Captain Alexander Kynoch of No. 37 Squadron took off from Stow Maries in his B.E.12. At the same time, Captain Henry Stroud of No. 61 Squadron – a former Royal Engineer who had been badly wounded in action in 1915 – departed Rochford in his S.E.5. Both pilots were climbing to intercept a bomber reportedly heading for London. Weather conditions at the time had caused most sorties to be cancelled, but the two flew on in total darkness. Over the village of Shotgate, the two aircraft collided, coming down in adjacent fields at Dollymans Farm. Local farmer William Wilson and his sister were first on the scene, where they found both pilots dead. Sometime later, Wilson erected two 'crosses', one at each site – both supposed to have been made from the propellers of the crashed aircraft. Despite having it written into his property's title deeds that both memorials should be 'forever held sacred', subsequent thefts saw the propeller taken from Kynoch's memorial and the other replaced on Stroud's. A bridge close to both, now spanning the A130 road, has since been named 'Monument Bridge'.

Less than a month after the collision between Kynoch and Stroud, the RFC and RNAS amalgamated to become the Royal Air Force (RAF). It was the world's largest air force,

Above left: Captain Alexander Kynoch's memorial at Dollymans Farm, Wickford, located close to that of Captain Henry Clifford Stroud. (Paul Bingley)

Above right: The memorial to Captain Henry Clifford Stroud, killed in a collision with Captain Alexander Kynoch over Shotgate in 1918. It was erected in 1920 on Dollymans Farm, close to the new A130. (Paul Bingley)

with 5,182 pilots in service. Eighty-four of those opposed the last German air raid on London, on 19 May 1918, when thirty-eight Gothas and three 'Giants' bombed parts of the capital, plus areas of Essex and Kent. Six of the Gothas were destroyed during the RAF's inaugural mission, including one by Lieutenant A. J. Arkell of RAF North Weald Bassett. Flying his Bristol F.2 fighter, nicknamed *Devil-in-the-Dark*, he shot down a Gotha over East Ham. It was the last enemy aircraft to be destroyed by an airman flying from Essex.

On 5 August 1918, the last German air raid on Britain took place. Five Zeppelins, including L.70, headed for the east coast of England. The Commander of L.70 was Fregattenkapitän Peter Strasser, the Führer der Luftschiffe – or 'Leader of Airships'. Major Egbert Cadbury, a member of the prominent industrial family, was swiftly on hand to intercept him. At 16,400 feet (5,000 metres), Cadbury's tracers ignited the airship's gas, turning it into a fireball. The Zeppelin immediately crashed close to Wells-next-the-Sea, killing Strasser and his crew. The next day, Cadbury wrote to his father:

> You will have heard probably before this reaches you that my lucky star has again been in the ascendant, and that another Zeppelin has gone to destruction, sent there by a perfectly peaceful live-and-let-live citizen, who has no lust for blood or fearful war spirit in his veins.

The peace-loving Cadbury need not have worried for long. Three months later, the First World War ended. Although 1,414 people had been killed and 3,410 injured in the first 'Blitz' on Great Britain, Essex, its aerodromes and airmen had risen to their first aerial challenge.

Chapter Two

Golden Age/Gathering Storm

Within months of Armistice Day, many of the RAF's Essex flight stations and landing grounds were closed. The wartime restriction on private flying, which had stood for almost five years, was then lifted. The 'golden age of aviation' was about to begin.

Soon after the end of hostilities, William Sholto Douglas, who had served as both a lieutenant in the British Army and a captain in the RFC, joined Handley Page Transport as a commercial pilot. On 1 May 1919, he flew eleven passengers from Cricklewood, London, to Manchester on the first post-war passenger flight in the country. Eleven days later, Sholto Douglas then appeared over Southend-on-Sea, where he circled the town's pier before dropping a small package containing copies of the latest edition of the *London Evening News*. His stunt was the first recorded civil aircraft movement over Essex following the end of the war.

Civil flying quickly proved to be a popular activity. Several months after Sholto Douglas's jaunt over Southend, the Navarro Aviation Company moved into the newly relinquished RAF aerodrome at Rochford – by then, the largest landing ground in Essex. The Central Aircraft Company arrived soon after and both businesses began offering pleasure flights over the town, Navarro using a converted military Avro 504K and

The Central Aircraft Company's Centaur IVB floated biplane, used for pleasure flights over Southend-on-Sea. The Navarro Aviation Company also used a converted Avro 504K at Rochford. (Authors' Collection)

Central employing its newly designed Centaur IVB floated biplane. Both were joined by other Avro 504Ks belonging to Surrey Flying Services, which also moved to Rochford in the summer of 1922.

When the Treaty of Versailles was signed on 28 June 1919, officially ending the war, twenty landing grounds in Essex remained in the hands of the Air Ministry. Six months later, Sutton's Farm was returned to agriculture. In late 1922, however, the Air Ministry again began looking for potential sites for new fighter aerodromes within a 20-mile radius of London. Although areas of land at Romford, Grays, Ockendon, Ingatestone and Orsett were all surveyed, North Weald Bassett and Sutton's Farm were judged to be the most suitable. Sutton's Farm was duly repurchased as a 'necessity for the defensive measures of England' and two years later reconstruction work began.

Even so, pleasure flying continued to attract the public. Frank Neale of Thornwood, Epping, saw its potential, becoming the first Essex man to take up 'joy-riding', using a solitary Avro 504K. Operating from several fields in north Essex, he then moved to Southend. W. G. Pudney of Canvey Island – another former soldier and RFC fighter pilot who hailed from Wellington, New Zealand – then established the Essex Aviation Company at Gidea Park, also using an ex-military 504K. Pudney became a highly respected pilot who later embarked on a perilous survey flight along the coast of West Africa in 1931 before returning to England to rejoin the RAF as one of its first test pilots.

By September 1927, the RAF had returned to North Weald Bassett. Officially opened and renamed RAF North Weald, the first fighters of No. 56 Squadron arrived two weeks later. Six months on (and almost four years after reconstruction had first begun), RAF Sutton's Farm was formally opened. It, too, was renamed (as RAF Hornchurch). The RAF's No. 111 Squadron, commanded by Squadron Leader Keith Park, arrived at Hornchurch shortly afterwards with a young airman among its ranks by the name of Pilot Officer Frank Whittle. He would go on to design the first turbojet engine.

Both North Weald and Hornchurch were opened as part of a new air defence system that extended from Duxford in Cambridgeshire to Devizes, Wiltshire. Part of the overall 'Air Defence of Great Britain', Essex's 'Metropolitan Royal Air Force' was given responsibility for a 15-mile-deep 'Aircraft Fighting Zone'. Together with the Royal Artillery and Observer Corps, the combination of services would allow fighters based at both Essex airfields enough time to counter any aerial threat posed to London.

The plan was put into mock effect on 28 June 1928, when five Armstrong Whitworth Siskin fighters of No. 111 Squadron sped across Essex to intercept a formation of eleven aircraft that had just flown non-stop from Rome. The Regia Aeronautica (Italian Air Force) aircraft were swiftly met and escorted into Hornchurch, just in time for their commanding officer, General Italo Balbo, to take part in an RAF pageant at Hendon.

The three squadrons based in Essex all took part in their own aerial display over Cranbrook Park, Ilford, two months later. The event was billed as the 'British Legion Carnival Fete', but its true aim was to raise funds for the RAF's continued expansion. This growth eventually led to the arrival of No. 54 Squadron at Hornchurch four months later. The new unit would remain at the Essex airfield for the next eleven years.

In the civil air sector, long-distance records were also being set. On 24 May 1930, Amy Johnson landed in Darwin, Australia, after a record-setting flight from Croydon. The next day, racing driver and speedboat racer Mrs Victor Bruce took her first flying lesson.

Born Mildred Mary Petre at Coptfold Hall, Margaretting, Bruce had already set records on land and in the water. Having been awarded her pilot's licence in July 1930, she purchased an all-metal Blackburn Bluebird IV biplane in an attempt to write her name into the aviation record books.

Taking off from Heston, Bruce flew east, where she braved oil leaks, monsoon rains and malaria. After flying across the Yellow Sea from China to Korea, she became the first person to achieve the feat. Then, twenty-five days after leaving Heston, she landed in Tokyo – the first person to successfully fly from England to Japan.

Bruce's journey continued across the Pacific Ocean by ship, followed by a further long-distance flight over the United States. Two crashes and another ocean-going voyage later, she circled over Lympne, Kent, before being escorted into land by Amy Johnson. 'Mrs Victor Bruce' of Essex had become the first person to fly around the world alone – albeit after crossing two oceans by ship.

Nine months later, Croydon-born Edward Hillman arrived at Maylands, near Romford, where he erected three large hangars, several workshops and a passenger reception complete with restaurant. Having operated a successful coach service between Romford and Clacton, Hillman – a keen pilot – obtained a licence for the new aerodrome, where he intended to enter into the airline business. On 1 April 1932, Hillman's Saloon Coaches & Airways Limited began a scheduled air service between the two Essex towns. What had once taken four hours by road would now take just thirty minutes by the company's new de Havilland DH.80 Puss Moth. The inaugural operation became Essex's first passenger air service.

Later that year, Maylands Aerodrome was enlarged to accommodate Hillman's growing air service. On 24 September, it was the location for the 'Essex Air Pageant', a festival which included a display of twenty different types of aircraft – among them, No. 54 Squadron's Bristol Bulldogs. The show attracted 20,000 spectators, who saw the 'official opening' of Hillman's aerodrome, attended by Amy Johnson.

Hillman subsequently replaced his Puss Moths with DH.83 Fox Moths, but he quickly pressed de Havilland into constructing a larger twin-engine version of the aircraft. On 12 November 1932, the prototype DH.84 Dragon flew its maiden flight. The following

Mildred Mary Petre, aka 'Mrs Victor Bruce', became the first person to fly around the world alone, using a Blackburn Bluebird IV aircraft nicknamed *Bluebird*. (Authors' Collection)

DH80A Puss Moth G-ABVX *Gilford* was one of the first aircraft put into service by Hillman's Airways at Maylands Aerodrome. (Authors' Collection)

month, Hillman's first Dragon arrived. On 20 December, Amy Johnson – who would eventually fly several services for Hillman's Airways – returned to Maylands, where she christened the new aircraft *Maylands* in honour of its base.

Despite this, a year later, Hillman purchased 180 acres of farmland on a twenty-five-year lease at Stapleford Tawney, where he set about constructing three hangars, a concrete apron and a passenger terminal. In June 1934, he transferred his entire operation from Maylands to the new aerodrome, which he named 'Essex Airport, Abridge'. The move was brought about by Hillman's Airways' growing fleet and expanding services, which now included services to Paris, Belfast and Glasgow.

Shortly after arriving at Stapleford, Hillman again turned to de Havilland to supply its newly developed DH.89 'Dragon Six' aircraft – a nine-seater, the faster and more comfortable successor to the DH.84 Dragon. The type entered commercial service with Hillman's Airways in the summer of 1934.

The first production Dragon Six, which subsequently became known as the Rapide, arrived at Stapleford in June. It was awarded its airworthiness certificate in July and assigned to Hillman's Paris route shortly afterwards. On 2 October 1934, six passengers boarded the aircraft at Stapleford just before 10 a.m. They were due to be flown to Paris by Flying Officer Walter Bannister, a former RAF second lieutenant. Less than an hour later, in poor weather conditions, the aircraft plunged into the English Channel 4 miles from Folkestone, killing all onboard. It was later found that Bannister's lack of experience in navigation and instrument flying had caused him to descend too low in a bid to find clearer weather. Although the accident failed to dent Hillman's reputation, it was the first accident involving the new type of aircraft.

By December 1934, Hillman's Airways was floated on the Stock Exchange, becoming a public company. The airline also picked up a lucrative contract delivering mail between London, Liverpool, Glasgow and Belfast. Sadly, however, Edward Hillman never lived to see the continued success of his venture. Less than a fortnight later, on New Year's Eve 1934, Hillman died at the age of forty-five. His death was attributed to his wartime service, which had seen him lose part of his leg at Mons, France, in 1918.

A 1934 advertisement for the Hillman's Airways Paris service from Stapleford Tawney depicts its prototype DH.84 Dragon. (Authors' Collection)

One of three Dragon Rapides now operating with Classic Wings at the Imperial War Museum, Duxford, TX310 *Nettie* was built in 1946 and was one of the last of the type to enter service. (Richard E. Flagg)

Shortly afterwards, control of Hillman's Airways passed to the Whitehall Securities Corporation, a financial investment firm with a growing interest in the airline business. Yet, despite the company's financial backing, another tragedy quickly followed.

On 21 February 1935, two American female passengers boarded one of Hillman's Airways' DH.84 Dragons at Stapleford. Captain John Kirton was set to fly both Elizabeth du Bois and her sister, Jane, to Paris Le Bourget. Daughters of the American Consul-General in Italy, Coert du Bois, the pair often travelled around Europe together. Although the Dragon had seats for six passengers, the wealthy sisters paid £21 to 'charter' the flight for themselves. Shortly after 10 a.m., the aircraft took off.

With no cabin attendants, it fell to the pilot to look after the welfare of his passengers. Unable to leave his seat, Kirton was approached by one of the sisters to close the cockpit door because of a draught. This he did, before turning the aircraft south towards France. Forty-five minutes later, he opened the door to check on his passengers. To his shock, he found their seats empty and the passenger entry door unfastened. Kirton alerted Croydon Aerodrome by radio and promptly returned to Stapleford.

By the time he landed, news of the incident had already come to the attention of the police. Two men working on a house in Park Drive, Upminster, had reported seeing an object fall from the sky just as an unseen aeroplane flew overhead. Hurrying to the scene at Rushmere Avenue, they found the sisters lying face-down holding each other. Both were dead. An inspection of the aircraft found a woman's shoe, a single suitcase, two handbags and two sealed letters. The letters revealed that the sisters had made a suicide pact following the deaths of their fiancés – two RAF officers who had been killed in a flying accident in Sicily just a week earlier. A verdict of suicide 'whilst the balance of the mind was disturbed' was later recorded by a coroner.

Hillman's Airways' trail of tragedies led to a change in fortunes for the airline and for British aviation in general. Less than six months later, Whitehall Securities merged the Essex airline with two others under its control – Spartan Air Lines of Heston and its sister company United Airways, based at Blackpool. The three became known as Allied British Airways in September 1935, before the name was changed to British Airways Ltd a month later. The new airline operated from Stapleford for several months, introducing a new Malmo route to its services, before moving all flights to Heston and, later, Gatwick. The county of Essex, therefore, had witnessed the birth of the UK's modern-day flag-carrier.

Shortly after British Airways Ltd departed Stapleford, British military aviation underwent a change of its own. In July 1936, the Air Defence of Great Britain was reformed into four new sectors: RAF Bomber Command, Fighter Command, Coastal Command and Training Command. Exercises then began taking place in conjunction with the Royal Observer Corps to test their combined reaction to an attacking force entering British airspace over the coast of south-east England.

The move came just four months after Germany had moved its forces into the Rhineland – a direct contravention of the Treaty of Versailles. This was preceded by an Italian invasion of Abyssinia (present-day Ethiopia). The heightened tensions across Europe saw recruiting targets for the Royal Air Force Volunteer Reserve (RAFVR) increased. A new Radio Direction Finding (RDF) system was also being trialled, while a barrage balloon scheme was put into effect. The RAF was beginning to expand at an increasing rate, and nowhere was this more evident than in the number of airfields then under construction.

In April 1937, a new fighter airfield was opened at Debden, near Saffron Walden. Thought to have been earmarked as a suitable flying site after a Bristol Bulldog made an emergency landing in 1935, the Gloster Gladiators of No. 87 Squadron arrived at the new airfield in June. The RAF's No. 65 Squadron at Hornchurch had already been equipped with the Gladiator when the airfield was visited by an unusual military mission five months later.

German generals Erhard Milch and Ernst Udet – both First World War aces – were shown 'the works' at Hornchurch by the RAF, including No. 65 Squadron's new Gloster Gladiators. According to one pilot, Robert Stanford Tuck (who would later go on to become a leading fighter ace), the pilots were warned by their station commander not to answer any questions about defensive tactics, operational control or the Gladiator's 'new reflector gunsight'. When Milch clambered up onto Tuck's aircraft to enquire about the weapon, Tuck informed him, as ordered, that he 'hadn't learnt how to use it'. Even so, an accompanying Air Vice Marshal promptly interjected and gave Milch a full explanation, including its advantages, disadvantages and settings. An appalled Tuck briefly considered suggesting that they give Milch one 'to take home as a souvenir'.

Milch had been a leading architect of the resurgent German air force, the Reichsluftwaffe, but the RAF was also bolstering its ranks. The response to the Air Ministry's call for volunteers to the RAFVR had seen its training schools flooded with new recruits. At Stapleford, No. 21 Elementary and Reserve Flying Training School (ERFTS) was established on 1 January 1938 to alleviate pressure on the other nine schools already in use. Using de Havilland Tiger Moths, No. 21 set about training its new students, including Loughton civil engineer J. E. 'Johnnie' Johnson. Like Robert Stanford Tuck, 'Johnnie' Johnson would become a fighter ace, and the RAF's eventual top-scoring pilot, with thirty-eight aerial victories to his name.

Five months after No. 21 ERFTS was established at Stapleford, the RAF's first monoplane fighter, the Hawker Hurricane, arrived at nearby North Weald. RAF No. 56 Squadron's pilots were soon putting the new fighter through its paces over Essex. Johnson was duly

A Gloster Gladiator of No. 87 Squadron being wheeled out of one of Debden's hangars in 1938. This still was taken from the British comedy movie *It's in the Air*, starring George Formby, which was partially filmed at Debden. (Authors' Collection)

warned by his flying instructor to 'keep a sharp look-out for those brutes... they come at you at a terrific speed and, head on, look no bigger than a razor blade'.

On 28 May 1938, the Hurricanes paraded over RAF Hornchurch for Empire Air Day. One of sixty RAF airfields and thirty civil aerodromes to open its doors during the event, it was an opportunity for the general public to see the Royal Air Force 'at home' and to inspect its equipment. Over 10,000 people turned up at Hornchurch, with many more lining the streets outside. Similar events took place at Debden, North Weald and the civil aerodrome at Rochford.

Several months later, the National Women's Air Reserve (a group that had been formed to provide aid during national emergencies) held 'The Great Women's Air Rally' at a rain-soaked Maylands Aerodrome. Pauline Gower, daughter of parliamentarian Sir Robert Gower, was one of the female pilots attending the rally, where she performed a 'strip-tease bombing', dropping bags of flour and female garments onto a car below. Over sixty passengers were also taken up on joyrides during the event, which turned out to be the last civil air display in Essex for seven years.

It was also to be Maylands' swansong as a civil aerodrome. Two months later, the aerodrome was deemed no longer safe due to a build-up of housing around its perimeter. Flying activities were transferred to a smaller aerodrome at Chigwell, which was officially opened on 24 September 1938.

A few miles further south, an area of farmland that had previously been used as a landing ground during the First World War was purchased by the City of London Corporation. The corporation's intention was to develop an area of Fairlop Plain as a 'major airport'. However, the deteriorating situation in Europe saw the project shelved. This instability led to all three Essex fighter stations being placed on full war alert. All aircraft were promptly camouflaged and placed at thirty minutes' readiness.

At North Weald, its four grass strips had been replaced by two permanent concrete runways and provided with night-landing facilities. The magnificence of its new look was there for all to see (at least for those who had a television set), when Nos 56 and 151 Squadrons carried out formation flying over the airfield for a British Broadcasting Corporation live outside broadcast on 19 October. It was the watching public's first chance to see the RAF in training.

Not to be outdone, Hornchurch witnessed a momentous event of its own on 13 February 1939, when the first Supermarine Spitfire landed in Essex. Allocated to No. 74 Squadron, further arrivals in March saw Nos 54 and 65 Squadrons equipped with the fighter. In due course, Hornchurch and its three Spitfire squadrons would become a vital facet of Fighter Command.

By August 1939, and with war on the horizon, Rochford (which had been engaged in the training of RAFVR pilots) was requisitioned altogether and placed in No. 11 Group of Fighter Command. Allocated as a forward satellite to Hornchurch, No. 54 Squadron's Spitfires arrived at the airfield on 11 August to begin their patrols over the North Sea.

Less than two weeks later, RAF personnel were recalled from leave. Station defence schemes were stepped up and buildings camouflaged. The nine fighter squadrons based at the four Essex airfields were about to face the world's strongest air force. The gathering storm had almost arrived.

CHAPTER THREE

Invasions

Fifty-four hours after German troops marched into Poland, Prime Minister Neville Chamberlain made an announcement to the British people. Britain had declared war on Germany. Thirty minutes later, an air-raid siren wailed across London. The capital was facing the threat of aerial bombardment once more.

The warning was a false alarm triggered by a French aircraft making its way across the coast. The next day, six Spitfires of No. 74 Squadron were scrambled from Hornchurch for the first time to intercept another unidentified aircraft. Again, it turned out to be a false alarm. It was a pattern that would be catastrophically repeated a few days later.

On 6 September 1939, a searchlight battery at Mersea Island wrongly identified a friendly aircraft crossing the Essex coastline. Hawker Hurricanes from North Weald were scrambled to investigate, but a technical fault with the new RDF station at Canewdon misidentified the Hurricanes as hostile. More fighters were despatched from North Weald, but they, too, were misidentified. The Spitfires of No. 74 Squadron were then detailed to engage the 'raid' and immediately took off from Hornchurch. Through a combination of 'miscommunication, inexperience and over-enthusiasm', two of the Spitfire pilots mistook the Hurricanes for German fighters and attacked, shooting two of them down. Pilot Officer Montague Hulton-Harrop was killed, becoming the first Fighter Command casualty of the Second World War. The other pilot, Frank Rose, managed to crash-land his aircraft in a nearby field.

The incident led to the arrests of the Spitfire pilots on their return to Hornchurch. A month later, Pilot Officer John Freeborn and Flying Officer Vincent 'Paddy' Byrne found themselves subject to court martial, although both were subsequently exonerated. The incident became known as the 'Battle of Barking Creek' and led to wholesale changes in Fighter Command's identification procedures.

While the RAF pilots grappled with their new-found situation, German bombers began carrying out minelaying operations in the North Sea. During one operation, on 30 April, a Heinkel He 111 was forced down below thick cloud off the coast of Clacton. It was then hit by anti-aircraft fire before crashing onto a house in Victoria Avenue, Clacton, killing its crew and two civilians. The explosion from unspent mines damaged fifty houses and injured 162 people. The county of Essex, therefore, became the scene of England's first fatal civilian casualties of the Second World War.

The first civilian deaths on the British mainland during the Second World War took place at Victoria Road, Clacton, on 30 April 1940. Frederick and Dorothy Gill were killed when a Heinkel He 111 crashed on their home. (Authors' Collection)

Auxiliary Air Force (AAF) units soon began arriving in Essex to bolster the hard-pressed RAF squadrons. Hornchurch's pilots had flown over 1,000 sorties since the outbreak of war, losing twenty-seven men in the process. Hornchurch's satellite airfield, Rochford, subsequently welcomed the Spitfires of No. 616 (AAF) Squadron, which arrived on 27 May 1940. As Pilot Officer Hugh Dundas approached the newly requisitioned site, he noted:

> There were two small hangars on the south side of the field, old fashioned buildings of the type which might have been put up during the First World War. There was a clubhouse in the south-east corner. There were no barrack blocks, parade grounds or other paraphernalia of a normal RAF station. This was a field which had been used as a centre for private flying enthusiasts, and was now pressed into war service.

A fellow pilot who took off from Rochford the following day was Flight Lieutenant Adolph 'Sailor' Malan of No. 74 Squadron. Malan, a South African, had been criticised for allegedly ordering the attack on No. 56 Squadron's Hurricanes during the 'Battle of Barking Creek'. Nevertheless, on 28 May, after achieving five 'kills' during the evacuation of Dunkirk, he was awarded the Distinguished Flying Cross (DFC).

Three weeks later, Malan was back in action over Essex. In an attempt to destroy the RDF facility at Canewdon, 2 miles north of Rochford, the Germans mistakenly struck Southend, killing one person and injuring twelve. Malan managed to pursue and hit two of the He 111s, one of which crashed in the garden of the Bishop of Chelmsford. As 'the first single-seater pilot of the war to destroy an enemy aircraft at night', Malan was awarded a bar to his DFC, which was presented to him by King George VI at Hornchurch a week later.

Owing to its strategic position close to London, and the fact that its squadrons were equipped entirely with Spitfires, Hornchurch was one of the most important of the 'sector' headquarters in No. 11 Group. When Adolf Hitler gave the Luftwaffe the order to destroy the RAF and its supporting infrastructure, Hornchurch was expected to be at the forefront of any action. Yet, it was Debden that suffered first.

Erroneously, Debden's air-raid alarm had first sounded on 18 June. However, forty-five days later, German bombs rained down on the airfield, destroying several buildings and killing five people. Weeks later, on the day that German bombs fell on London for the first time, both Hornchurch and North Weald were attacked by the Luftwaffe. Hornchurch was left with eighty-five craters and damaged telephone lines, while the latter was struck by over 200 bombs, severely damaging its married quarters and killing nine members of the Essex Regiment.

Relentless German attacks followed over the next few days. On 26 August, an estimated 170 German aircraft flew along the Thames Estuary before being intercepted by RAF fighters. Six Dornier Do 17 bombers managed to escape the fighter defences and make it to Debden, where they caused substantial damage resulting in five deaths. Rochford was also attacked, although one Do 17, which had been badly damaged by a Spitfire from Hornchurch, made a wheels-up landing on the airfield. Its crew of three were immediately captured and the largely intact aircraft was recovered by the War Office for closer inspection.

The German attacks were not only affecting the Essex airfields' ability to function (Debden's Sector Operations Room had to be relocated to Saffron Walden Grammar School due to severe damage), but the RAF pilots were also suffering. On 30 August, the Luftwaffe carried out 1,310 sorties leaving forty British fighters destroyed and nine pilots dead. The next day, Pilot Officer William Hodgson, a New Zealander with No. 85 Squadron at Debden, was scrambled to intercept 200 German aircraft approaching the Essex coast. After successfully destroying a Messerschmitt Me 109 and damaging a Do 17, Hodgson's Hurricane was hit. With his engine on fire, Hodgson 'side-slipped' his aircraft to extinguish the flames. Realising the situation was hopeless, he began preparing to bail out. Noticing a heavily populated area below, he then steered his Hurricane towards a field where he crash-landed. Hodgson was awarded the DFC for his actions. Six months later, however, he was killed in a flying accident near RAF Debden. The residents of Shotgate unveiled a memorial close to where he had previously crash-landed and named a road, Hodgson Way, in his honour.

By September 1940, another Essex airfield was handed to the RAF. Stapleford Tawney – once home to Hillman's Airways – saw the arrival of No. 46 Squadron's Hawker Hurricanes. Almost immediately, they were scrambled to head off an attack on nearby North Weald. As the Bristol Blenheims of No. 25 Squadron took off from North Weald's runways to avoid the raid, the Hurricanes mistook them for German bombers and fired. One Blenheim crashed, killing the pilot, while two others force-landed in farmland close to the airfield.

With the increasing frequency of raids, Essex airfields saw the comings and goings of new units. A 'special duties' squadron was formed at North Weald and equipped with two Westland Lysanders; its role was to make clandestine flights in support of resistance movements in Nazi-occupied territory. However, the persistent German attacks soon forced the squadron to move to Stapleford Tawney.

This marble tablet commemorates the heroism of Pilot Officer William Hodgson, who avoided crashing his damaged Hurricane on the village of Shotgate during the Battle of Britain. (Richard E. Flagg)

One of the squadrons already using the airfield was No. 151. Then in the process of being transferred to Digby in Lincolnshire, some of its Hurricanes had remained in Essex to continue daytime patrols. On 4 September, as one of them departed for a ferry flight to Digby, it struck a crane parked next to the runway. The aircraft instantly burst into flames and crashed, killing its pilot, Richard Ambrose, who was later buried at Epping Cemetery.

Three days after Ambrose's accident, the British government issued the codeword 'Cromwell', bringing the country's air, land and sea defences to their highest possible alert. An invasion was expected at any time. Nevertheless, the RAF continued to fend off the Luftwaffe, bringing down as many as fifty-six enemy aircraft in one day. Hornchurch's squadrons alone had accounted for 411 enemy aircraft destroyed and 235 'probables' since the outbreak of war.

Even so, further effort was required to accommodate the swelling RAF ranks now in Essex. On 26 September construction work began on an area of land close to the former RFC landing ground at Hainault Farm. Three concrete runways and accommodation for 1,200 airmen would eventually be built on the site before the newly named RAF Fairlop opened.

As Luftwaffe air raids on London intensified during October, the pilots of No. 46 Squadron at Stapleford faced their own mortality on a daily basis. On 15 October, around 400 German bombers approached London to deliver 530 tons of high explosives. Pilot Officer Peter Gunning engaged a number of escorting Me 109s 20,000 feet (6,000 metres) above the Thames Estuary. During a frantic dogfight, his Hurricane was damaged by cannon fire and crashed into a chalk pit close to Thurrock, with Gunning still at the controls. As with William Hodgson, Thurrock's residents unveiled a memorial to Peter Gunning and later named Gunning Road in his honour.

A similar fate befell one of Gunning's fellow No. 46 Squadron pilots just ten days later. Taking off from Stapleford Tawney to join a patrol north of Biggin Hill, Pilot Officer William Pattullo's Hurricane was 'bounced' by a German fighter and badly damaged. It was thought that Pattullo was attempting an emergency landing at Maylands Golf Course, near Romford, when his aircraft crashed onto a house in Woodstock Avenue, Harold Park.

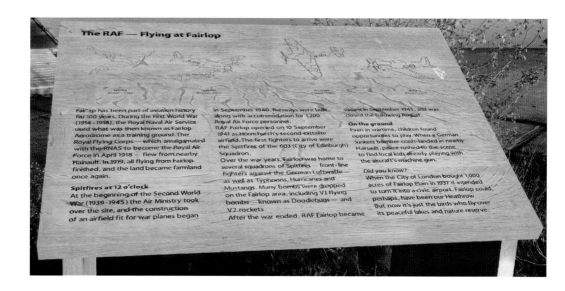

The RAF — Flying at Fairlop

Fairlop has been part of aviation history for 100 years. During the First World War (1914 - 1918), the Royal Naval Air Service used what was then known as Fairlop Aerodrome as a training ground. The Royal Flying Corps — which amalgamated with the RNAS to become the Royal Air Force in April 1918 — flew from nearby Hainault. In 1919, all flying from Fairlop finished, and the land became farmland once again.

Spitfires at 12 o'clock
At the beginning of the Second World War (1939-1945) the Air Ministry took over the site, and the construction of an airfield fit for war planes began

in September 1940. Runways were built, along with accommodation for 1,200 Royal Air Force personnel. RAF Fairlop opened on 10 September 1941 as Hornchurch's second satellite airfield. The first fighters to arrive were the Spitfires of the 603 (City of Edinburgh) Squadron. Over the war years, Fairlop was home to several squadrons of Spitfires — front-line fighters against the German Luftwaffe — as well as Typhoons, Hurricanes and Mustangs. Many bombs were dropped on the Fairlop area, including V1 flying bombs — known as Doodlebugs — and V2 rockets. After the war ended, RAF Fairlop became

vacant in September 1945, and was closed the following August.

On the ground
Even in wartime, children found opportunities to play. When a German Junkers bomber crash-landed in nearby Hainault, police rushed to the scene to find local kids already playing with the aircraft's machine gun.

Did you know?
When the City of London bought 1,000 acres of Fairlop Plain in 1937 it intended to turn it into a civic airport. Fairlop could, perhaps, have been our Heathrow. But now it's just the birds who fly over its peaceful lakes and nature reserve.

IN HONOURED MEMORY OF
Pilot Officer Peter Stackhouse Gunning, RAF
Aged 29
One of the Few
46 Sqn, Royal Air Force

PO⊙G

Whose Hawker Hurricane Mk1 aircraft N2480, fell to earth just beyond this spot into the then, Globe Quarry Chalk Pit, at around 13.00hrs on 15th October 1940 during the Battle of Britain, following a furious dog fight over the Dartford/Thurrock area at 20,000ft with the Messerschmitt 109 fighters of Major Adolf Galland's JG26.
Gunning Road was named in his honour and this plaque is placed out of respect by the residents of this community.
22nd October 2011

Above: RAF Fairlop's time as a Fighter Command airfield is now reflected in this wooden information board at Fairlop Waters. (Authors' Collection)

Left: Another Essex Battle of Britain memorial, commemorating Pilot Officer Peter Gunning, whose Hurricane crashed into a chalk pit close to Grays. Gunning Road was named in his honour. (Richard E. Flagg)

Although he was rescued from the wreckage, Pattullo died from his injuries the next day. He was later buried at St Andrews Church, North Weald.

By now, Rochford had become a station in its own right and was allocated full satellite status. It was also renamed RAF Southend. Stapleford Tawney, on the other hand, was declared unserviceable two weeks later due to a wet autumn. All flying activity ceased at the airfield for the next year. Nevertheless, what Churchill described as the 'Battle of Britain' was finally over. Although night bombing raids on London and other British cities continued, it was estimated that 1,733 German aircraft had been destroyed.

Having attracted a number of German bombers during the Battle of Britain, Debden drew two extraordinary visits at the start of 1941. On 28 January, King George VI and Queen Elizabeth travelled to the station for an inspection. Six days later, a German He 111 bomber made an equally eye-opening arrival.

William 'Billy' Pattullo was just twenty-one years of age when his Hurricane crashed onto a house in Harold Park, Romford. The crash site at Keiray House is now marked by this plaque. (Richard E. Flagg)

After landing at Debden and taxiing to the watch office, one of its crew members jumped out and approached an RAF officer to ask where they were. He did so in German. Immediately realising the gravity of his error, he raced back to his aircraft, which rapidly swung round and took off. Despite the best attempts of the watch officer to raise the alarm, the panicked Germans made good their escape.

The British people were never immune to such 'visits'. On 19 April, just as a darts match was getting underway at the Prince of Wales pub in Chigwell, a lone German bomber flew overhead, releasing several parachute mines that slowly descended down. An estimated 1,000 kg (2,205 lb) of explosives ripped through the pub, destroying it and several adjacent houses. The resultant death toll was put at forty-six, but it was thought that over 120 were killed. Twenty of them were buried in a communal grave in St Mary's Church, Chigwell. In 1996, a plaque was unveiled by the parish council at the site of the tragedy.

Although the United States was yet to enter the war, there was no shortage of American volunteers to help protect the British public. By June 1941, the RAF's No. 71 Squadron had arrived at North Weald with its Hawker Hurricanes. They were flown by Americans who eventually made up the first of three RAF 'Eagle' squadrons – units that would merge to become an iconic fighter group that remained in Essex until the end of the war.

By September 1941, the Air Ministry Directorate General of Works had finished conducting a survey of additional airfield sites in eastern England. Some 180 new airfields had been proposed, including the remodelling of a number of existing sites. Bradwell Bay was already under construction, while Fairlop was declared operational on 10 September. A month later, work began on the construction of another site near Ridgewell.

Left: Erected in 1996, this stone monolith with plaque commemorates the night of 19 April 1941, when a German parachute mine landed on the Prince of Wales pub in Chigwell. (Paul Cannon)

Below: RAF Bradwell Bay's watch office, now a house, pictured in 2007. This Essex airfield was the only British fighter station to use the Fog Investigation and Dispersal Operation (FIDO). (Richard E. Flagg)

After the Japanese attack on Pearl Harbor and America's subsequent declaration of war on Germany, the need for new airfields in Britain took on greater urgency. Construction work soon began at Great Sampford, where trees and hedges were cut down to make way for a perimeter track, hardstands and accommodation for over 800 airmen. One week later, President Franklin D. Roosevelt officially announced that US forces would be stationed in Great Britain.

By May 1942, elements of the United States Army Air Forces' (USAAF) newly established 8th Air Force had arrived in England. It was for the Americans that Essex airfields were now being planned, constructed and opened.

Pictured in 2009, this taxiway is one of the few remnants of RAF Great Sampford. Briefly home to No. 133 Squadron – one of the famed 'Eagle' squadrons – Great Sampford's combat life was short. (Richard E. Flagg)

In early June, Ridgewell and Earls Colne joined a list of twenty-eight British airfields that were to be transferred from the RAF to the 8th Air Force. They were required to accommodate the 3,700 aircraft then scheduled for American fighter and bomber operations. However, it was calculated that up to 127 airfields would eventually be required, many of which were still to be constructed. Nevertheless, a unique construction was about to begin.

In July 1942, the 819th Engineer Battalion (Aviation) of the US Army arrived in the village of Great Saling. When their work was done, it would become the first British airfield built entirely by American troops. The site of foreigners tearing up the Essex countryside quickly drew scorn from some locals, as one engineer observed: 'They knew we were there to ruin their land – and when we had ruined it, we would then fly hundreds of aeroplanes from the base and low over their homes.'

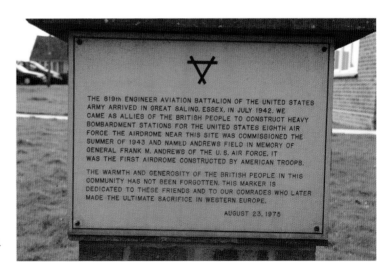

A marker stone in the village of Great Saling is dedicated to the first British airfield built by American troops – Andrews Field. Areas of the former airfield remain in use for private flying. (Richard E. Flagg)

THE 819th ENGINEER AVIATION BATTALION OF THE UNITED STATES ARMY ARRIVED IN GREAT SALING, ESSEX, IN JULY 1942. WE CAME AS ALLIES OF THE BRITISH PEOPLE TO CONSTRUCT HEAVY BOMBARDMENT STATIONS FOR THE UNITED STATES EIGHTH AIR FORCE. THE AIRDROME NEAR THIS SITE WAS COMMISSIONED THE SUMMER OF 1943 AND NAMED ANDREWS FIELD IN MEMORY OF GENERAL FRANK M. ANDREWS OF THE U. S. AIR FORCE. IT WAS THE FIRST AIRDROME CONSTRUCTED BY AMERICAN TROOPS.

THE WARMTH AND GENEROSITY OF THE BRITISH PEOPLE IN THIS COMMUNITY HAS NOT BEEN FORGOTTEN. THIS MARKER IS DEDICATED TO THESE FRIENDS AND TO OUR COMRADES WHO LATER MADE THE ULTIMATE SACRIFICE IN WESTERN EUROPE.

AUGUST 23, 1975

Chapter Four

Fields of America

Shortly after Great Saling's construction had begun, Earls Colne's was complete. Essex's first heavy bomber airfield, although allocated to the 8th Air Force, was temporarily handed to RAF Bomber Command. Even so, there were no British squadrons available to use it. Instead, its three intersecting runways remained largely inactive – except for the emergency landing of a damaged B-17 Flying Fortress two months later.

Erected by a local family in 2006, this impressive memorial commemorates the British and American units that served at RAF Earls Colne between May 1943 and April 1946. (Richard E. Flagg)

Wethersfield was another Essex site allocated to the 8th Air Force. Construction had begun almost at the same time as Great Saling, but a shortage of men and materials had interrupted its construction shortly after the runways had been laid. It was another year before Wethersfield turned fully operational, making it the longest gestation period for any Essex airfield during the Second World War.

By now, other Essex sites had been allocated to the 8th Air Force. Birch and Matching were earmarked as fighter airfields, while Boreham, Boxted, Chipping Ongar, Gosfield, Great Dunmow, Hadstock, Rivenhall and Stansted Mountfitchet were all assigned as bomber bases. Several others were also tentatively reserved, including Beaumont, Cold Norton, High Roding, Ingatestone and Southminster.

On 16 August 1942, construction work began at Gosfield. Located next to a field that had once been used as a night landing ground by the RFC, the level site was found to be ideal. Tented accommodation was quickly erected by the 816th Engineer Battalion (Aviation), but with the airfield construction programme falling further behind schedule, most of the American troops were transferred to the more advanced construction site at Great Saling.

By September 1942, Bradwell Bay (which had been established as a landing ground for aircraft carrying out bombing runs over the Dengie Flats) turned operational. The RAF's No. 23 Squadron arrived with its de Havilland Mosquitoes before going on to pioneer long-range intruder flights over Nazi-occupied Europe.

No. 133 Squadron – one of the three American 'Eagle' squadrons – was then transferred to the newly opened Great Sampford. Now equipped with four blister hangars and two mesh wire runways, the airfield was soon reverberating to the sound of Nos 133, 676 and 65 Squadrons' Spitfires – the latter being an 'Essex-born' unit that had been established in 1934.

Although RAF Gosfield was decommissioned in 1946, parts of it still remain. The original control tower has since been extended and modified for use as an industrial and office unit. (Richard E. Flagg)

No. 133 Squadron's tenure at Great Sampford was short-lived, however. Debden was transferred to the 8th Air Force as a fighter station on 12 September – the same day that the 4th Fighter Group of the 8th Air Force was established. The RAF 'Eagle' squadrons were all absorbed into the 4th and transferred to Debden, collectively becoming known as the 'Debden Eagles'. Three days later, William Sholto Douglas – by now Air Officer Commander-in-Chief of Fighter Command – handed over the three squadrons to the Commander of the 8th Air Force, Major General Carl Spaatz, remarking:

> We, of Fighter Command, deeply regret the parting. In the course of the past 18 months we have seen the stuff of which you are made. We could not ask for better companions with whom to see this fight through to the finish... we shall watch your future with confidence.

Debden quickly became the 'showpiece' of the 8th Air Force's fighter airfields. A month later, First Lady Eleanor Roosevelt visited the airfield on a tour of Great Britain. The rudimentary facilities on offer had been vastly improved by the opening of an American Red Cross canteen. 'There is no other place for the boys to go nearby,' she wrote in her diary, 'so the movies and dances and "eats" offered... are very much appreciated.'

By December 1942, the so-called 'Friendly Invasion' was well underway. A mansion near Earls Colne was taken over by the United States Army Air Forces (USAAF) on land requisitioned from the Marks Hall estate. Part of the estate's deer park had also been commandeered to build RAF Earls Colne. Marks Hall would become the nerve-centre for Essex's strategic and tactical bombing operations over the next eighteen months.

Other sites previously allocated to the 8th Air Force were then relinquished altogether. Cold Norton, Beaumont, High Roding, Ingatestone and Southminster all had their construction plans postponed in mid-December. Later that same month, however, RAF Ridgewell finally turned operational.

Over a million man hours, a million cubic yards of concrete, 6 miles of water mains, 24 miles of drains and more than 500 buildings had gone into constructing Ridgewell. Yet

Former RAF 'Eagle' pilots swarm their P-47s around Debden's main runway in preparation for a 4th Fighter Group mission over Holland in May 1943. (Authors' Collection)

RAF Ridgewell, Essex's only long-term heavy bomber base, was largely erased from the landscape in the 1960s. Since then, long sections of its perimeter track have been put to use as public roads. (Richard E. Flagg)

although the airfield had been allocated to the Americans, it was immediately handed to a homeless RAF squadron. On 29 December, the Short Stirlings of No. 90 Squadron began circling the new airfield. The first bomber to land promptly swung off the main runway and damaged its undercarriage. Ridgewell's career as 'Essex's only long-term heavy bomber base' was off to an inauspicious start.

In January 1943, following an Allied conference held in Morocco, the 'Casablanca Directive' was issued. Its aim was to meld the RAF and USAAF into one air arm to bring about 'the progressive destruction and dislocation of the German military, industrial and economic system'. It had been agreed that the RAF would bomb by night and the USAAF by day. On 25 February, the 'round-the-clock' strategic bombing of Nazi-occupied Europe began.

Just after seven o'clock in the evening, eleven Halifax bombers of RAF No. 102 (Ceylon) Squadron began taking off from RAF Pocklington, Yorkshire. Joining up with another 326 RAF bombers, their intended target was the German city of Nuremberg. Almost an hour into the flight, the bombers began encountering severe weather conditions which caused heavy icing. Two of the aircraft turned back, while a third span out of control and crashed into a field near Ardleigh, exploding on impact. The accident killed its crew of seven and left a crater 90 feet (27 metres) wide. It also caused damage to a number of nearby farm buildings and set two haystacks on fire. Ninety minutes later, an unexploded 1,000 lb (453 kg) bomb then blew up, injuring two firemen. Like similar incidents throughout the Second World War, residents unveiled a memorial detailing the crash of the Halifax, while highlighting other events that took place in and around Ardleigh during both world wars.

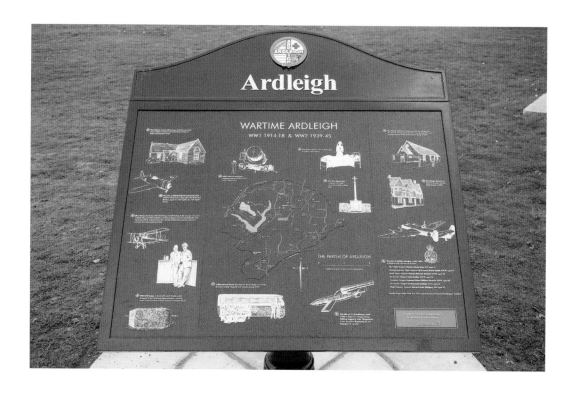

Above: In September 2018, a specially commissioned sign detailing Ardleigh's wartime past was unveiled. It pinpoints eleven sites around the village that came to prominence as a result of both world wars. (Richard E. Flagg)

Left: An aerial shot of the 387th Bombardment Group's B-26 Marauders on the ground at RAF Chipping Ongar, taken from an overflying B-17 Flying Fortress in the summer of 1943. (Authors' Collection)

With Gosfield and Great Saling still under construction, the next Essex airfield to turn operational was RAF Chipping Ongar. Originally allocated as a heavy bomber airfield, it would go through several reallocations before becoming the home of a medium bomb group.

By now, the Republic P-47 Thunderbolt had arrived in the skies over Essex. On 8 March 1943 the fighter – nicknamed 'The Jug' (due to its resemblance as a milk bottle) – was soon escorting American bombers over Europe. Two days later, the P-47s of the 4th Fighter

Group took off from Debden on their first operational mission – a 'fighter sweep' over France to lure the Luftwaffe into air-to-air combat. Although the P-47s' role was to closely guard the American bombers, the fighters would eventually be sent ahead of formations to find, fight and destroy any enemy aircraft before they could reach them.

The growing number of American aircraft now appearing over Essex failed to prevent the Germans from following suit. On 13 March, Bradwell Bay came under attack by several Junkers Ju 88s, one of which was shot down over Burnham-on-Crouch by anti-aircraft fire. The next day, the Germans returned, although their bombs fell short of the airfield. Reprisal raids on German airfields in France quickly followed. These were carried out by the next new fighters to arrive in Essex.

On 6 April 1943, two Hawker Typhoon squadrons arrived at RAF Fairlop. Almost immediately, they began taking part in low-level ground attacks on German airfields using aircraft fitted with two 1,000 lb (453 kg) bombs slung beneath each wing. The Typhoons would also be used to attack French sites believed to be constructing German long-range rockets – weapons that would later be used against Great Britain, and that would see the Typhoon become a key adversary.

New challengers to the 4th Fighter Group arrived at Debden a week later, when four of the 56th Fighter Group's P-47s landed at the Essex airfield. The two groups would become intense rivals throughout the war as they bid to become the top-scoring American fighter unit. Nevertheless, the 4th's pilots would always maintain a sense of superiority, having been allowed to retain the RAF's 'wings' on the right side of their new American tunics. The group's motto also proudly proclaimed: 'The Fourth but First.' Just two days later, as if to emphasise the point, the 4th scored the very first P-47 aerial victory over a German Focke-Wulf Fw 190.

With the burgeoning American presence and more airfields turning operational across Essex, a new US Army hospital was opened in the grounds of a large country house near Braintree. On 29 April 1943, White Court Park became the US Army 12th Evacuation Hospital. Built to provide a medical service for the increasing numbers of American airmen throughout Essex, the hospital was initially equipped with 750 beds, largely housed in Nissen huts. The site was subsequently expanded, particularly after D-Day, when its capacity was increased to over 800 beds.

Five days before the new hospital was opened, RAF Great Saling was officially unveiled by six American generals. However, just nine days after its opening, the Commanding General of the United States Forces in the European Theatre of Operations, Lieutenant General Frank M. Andrews, was killed in a B-24 Liberator accident during an inspection tour of Iceland. It was fitting, therefore, that the first airfield built by the US Army should be renamed in his honour. Great Saling duly became RAF Andrews Field – the only American-built airfield in England to be named after an individual.

Another site to see its identity change was Hadstock. Originally allocated as a bomber airfield in 1942, its construction had begun in May 1943. By this time, its name had been changed to Little Walden. Nevertheless, it would be a further ten months before the first American aircraft landed.

On 12 May, the B-17 Flying Fortresses of the 94th Bombardment Group arrived at Earls Colne, becoming the first American bombers to land in Essex. That same day, a US Army engineering battalion arrived at Boreham to begin construction of its bomber airfield.

White Court is a residential housing estate on the outskirts of Braintree. Built on the site of a wartime US Army hospital, the estate's past is commemorated by this brick-built memorial, unveiled on the fiftieth anniversary of American operations. (Richard E. Flagg)

Now a contemporary four-bedroom home, RAF Little Walden's control tower has undergone a useful transformation. Nevertheless, the airfield, closed in 1958, retains very little of its wartime past. (Richard E. Flagg)

The 620-acre site between the villages of Boreham and Little Waltham required the removal of 86 acres of woodland before its three intersecting runways, fifty hardstands and camps for 2,658 airmen could be built. Boreham was one of sixty-six airfields then under construction for the USAAF across Great Britain.

Andrews Field was the next Essex airfield to welcome the Americans, when the 96th Bombardment Group arrived with its B-17s from Grafton Underwood in Northamptonshire.

Another control tower remains at the former RAF Boreham, which is now a quarry. Pictured in 2012, the building was in use with the National Police Air Service as an operations control centre, until it was relocated in 2018. The tower is now earmarked for demolition as the quarry expands. (Richard E. Flagg)

Two days later, the group carried out its first and only mission from Essex – a raid on a naval storage depot at Rennes in France – before moving on to Snetterton Heath, Norfolk.

Five days later, the first American airmen began arriving at RAF Ridgewell. Over 2,000 men of the 381st Bombardment Group unloaded at Great Yeldham station after a lengthy journey from Colorado. Shortly afterwards, the group's B-17s landed at the airfield, which had already seen fifty-one operations carried out by RAF No. 90 Squadron's Short Stirlings. Much like No. 90 Squadron's unpromising arrival at Ridgewell, however, one of the first B-17s to land suffered a collapsed undercarriage on touchdown.

By now, RAF Boxted had turned operational with the arrival of the first medium bombers in Essex. The Martin B-26 Marauders of the 386th Bombardment Group arrived on 10 June from their previous base at Snetterton Heath, Norfolk. Although the 386th's stay at Boxted was brief, the group would remain in Essex for the next seventeen months.

As more American groups began arriving in Essex, so the jostling for permanent bases increased. The county saw numerous arrivals and transfers, the most notable of which was the departure of the 94th from Earls Colne on 13 June. Its task was to carry out an attack on Kiel in Germany before returning to a new base at Bury St Edmunds, Suffolk. On the return to England, however, the 94th was within sight of the Norfolk coast when twelve Ju 88s attacked. Nine B-17s were shot down, bringing its cumulative losses to seventeen after just two months in combat.

With inexperienced airmen and an influx of crews working on airfields still under construction, it was a matter of time before the first major accident took place. On 23 June 1943 – the day after the 381st's first mission from RAF Ridgewell – the group was preparing for its second bombing raid over Europe. As its B-17s were being loaded with 300 lb (136 kg) fused bombs, one of the bombers blew up on its hardstand. Two explosions left twenty-four men dead, including a British civilian who was cycling past. In terms of

Although still used for private aviation, RAF Boxted – an airfield once used by the two most successful USAAF fighter groups – is now a shadow of its former self. (Richard E. Flagg)

The aftermath of what was arguably the 8th Air Force's deadliest ground accident during the Second World War. Even today, fragments of the B-17 once known as *Caroline* are still being unearthed. (Authors' Collection)

loss of life, it was the 8th Air Force's deadliest ground accident to occur during the Second World War. Seventy-one years later, a memorial listing those who were killed was unveiled by members of the Ridgewell Airfield Commemorative Museum.

In July 1943, both Chipping Ongar and Great Dunmow went operational. A month later, the 816th Engineer Battalion returned to RAF Gosfield from Andrews Field to complete the former's unfinished construction. Stansted Mountfitchet was also selected to become

An aerial view of the former RAF Great Dunmow, taken in 2017. Over 10,000 trees were removed from the Easton Lodge estate to make way for the airfield, which closed just five years later. (Richard E. Flagg)

London Stansted Airport's terminal building, pictured from the air in 2016. Formerly known as RAF Stansted Mountfitchet, this once major USAAF airfield was a maintenance and supply depot. (Richard E. Flagg)

an advance air depot servicing bases across Essex. Equipped with extra hangars and hardstands, what would later become London's third international airport was opened for business on 7 August 1943.

By late September, the 8th Air Force had already carried out its 100th mission from England. On its 103rd, on 26 September, its bombers attacked several factories in the Paris area. As usual, many of the aircraft were returning over the English Channel before heading across Essex towards their bases in East Anglia. Two B-17s of the 385th Bombardment Group, based at RAF Great Ashfield, Suffolk, were overflying West Horndon when one suddenly flew out of control, slicing the other in two. *Dorsal Queen* went into a flat spin before slamming belly-down in a ditch, while *Raunchy Wolf* nose-dived into the ground. Seconds later *Dorsal Queen* exploded, killing the ten men onboard. There was just one survivor – its tail gunner, who had miraculously survived the severed tail's descent. Seventy-five years on, West Horndon Parish Council unveiled a memorial bench to honour the twenty-one airmen killed.

By October 1943, Gosfield's construction was almost complete. Eleven miles south-east, Birch's was about to begin. The 846th Engineer Battalion of the US Army arrived to begin construction of what eventually turned out to be Essex's (and the UK's) last airfield to be built by a battalion of the US Army.

By mid-October, the 8th Air Force was joined in England by the 9th Air Force, which had been transferred from the Middle East. Boreham, Andrews Field, Chipping Ongar, Great Dunmow and Stansted Mountfitchet were all reallocated to the 9th. Eleven others quickly followed. The groups based at these airfields were subsequently tasked with 'tactical' bombing – primarily, the air support of Allied ground forces.

This beautifully carved bench in West Horndon Park was unveiled in 2018. It commemorates the crews of *Dorsal Queen* and *Raunchy* Wolf – two B-17s that collided over the village on 26 September 1943. (Richard E. Flagg)

Boxted welcomed a new type of aircraft in November 1943 when the North American Aviation P-51 Mustangs of the 354th Fighter Group arrived. This new long-range escort fighter would prove pivotal to the success of Allied bombing operations. The 354th was the first to be equipped with the fighter, ultimately becoming known as 'The Pioneer Mustang Group'.

The next Essex airfield to turn operational was Wormingford. Although construction was still ongoing, the P-47s of the 9th Air Force's 362nd Fighter Group arrived at Wormingford on 30 November 1943. Ten days later, however, the Luftwaffe also appeared over Essex.

On 10 December several Essex bases received direct hits from German bombers in the heaviest bombardment of British airfields since Debden in 1940. Bombs straddled Birch's new runways, while Andrews Field also received minor damage. Yet it was Gosfield that was most heavily hit. Four American servicemen were killed when their hut was sprayed with cannon fire. Six weeks later, Hornchurch was bombed for the first time in three years when the Luftwaffe returned to carry out what soon became known as the 'Baby Blitz'.

By the turn of 1944, several newly constructed airfields were opened across Essex. On 22 January – the day after Hornchurch was bombed – RAF Rivenhall became the latest Essex airfield to welcome the Americans. Arriving from RAF Keevil in Wiltshire, the 363rd Fighter Group was the third unit to be equipped with the P-51. Four days later, RAF Matching saw the arrival of the 391st Bombardment Group and its B-26 Marauders.

The first of three 9th Air Force light bomb groups then arrived in England when the 416th and its new Douglas A-20 Havocs landed at RAF Wethersfield on 1 February 1944. A week

Major James H. Howard of the 354th Fighter Group at Boxted climbs into his P-51 Mustang. He became the only fighter pilot in the European Theater of Operations to receive the Medal of Honor. (Authors' Collection)

The silhouette of a P-51 Mustang on the wall of a building at Wormingford. Initially used as an RFC landing ground during the First World War, it was assigned as a USAAF fighter station in 1943. (Richard E. Flagg)

A door at Rivenhall bearing the name of an American commander. Having served primarily as a USAAF fighter station during the Second World War, Rivenhall has since become a quarry. (Richard E. Flagg)

RAF Matching's former control tower still stands today, seventy-five years after it was first built. The airfield was used as a bomber base by elements of the USAAF and RAF before closing in 1946. (Richard E. Flagg)

later, Stansted Mountfitchet (which had welcomed its first American ground crews in August 1943) finally saw the arrival of its first operational aircraft when the B-26 Marauders of the 344th Bombardment Group landed. They arrived on the day that the 323rd Bombardment Group at Earls Colne celebrated becoming the first B-26 unit to complete 100 missions.

Nevertheless, the P-51 was becoming a key weapon for the Allies. The new fighter had accounted for more enemy aircraft in just one month than in the previous two years combined. A number had been brought into service with the RAF and on 28 February Wing Commander Reginald Grant, of RAF No. 65 Squadron, took off in his from Gravesend, Kent, to escort a formation of bombers on a mission to attack a German rocket site in northern France.

The New Zealander, who had previously flown Spitfires from RAF Manston and received a DFC with bar, suffered engine problems shortly after take-off. At a height of 2,500 feet (762 metres), his P-51 began to roll and spiral down. Grant was seen to abandon the aircraft, which crashed close to Barrington's Farm, Orsett. Either overcome by fumes or too low for his parachute to fully deploy, Grant was killed when he struck the ground. Sixty years later, a brass plaque was unveiled in the grounds of Orsett fire station, close to where he lost his life.

On 4 March 1944, P-51s from the 4th Fighter Group at Debden made it over the German capital, Berlin, for the first time. However, the 363rd Fighter Group, flying from Rivenhall, lost eleven of its P-51s during the Luftwaffe's most successful day in combat against the new fighter.

The inherent dangers of huge numbers of aircraft flying over Essex was brought into sharp focus four days later, when two B-26s of the 344th Bombardment Group from

IN GRATEFUL MEMORY OF
WING COMMANDER
REGINALD JOSEPH COWAN GRANT. DFC AND BAR. DFM.
(RNZAF) 65 SQUADRON RAF.
WHO LOST HIS LIFE NEAR THIS SPOT IN DEFENCE OF THE UNITED KINGDOM
28TH FEBRUARY 1944
'FROM THE UTTERMOST ENDS OF THE EARTH'
LEST WE FORGET

Above: Wethersfield's layout remains largely intact thanks to its almost continuous use since the end of the Second World War. Today, the Ministry of Defence Police uses the site as its headquarters. (Richard E. Flagg)

Left: Unveiled in 2004, this discreet memorial recognises the sacrifice of Wing Commander Reginald Grant, whose Mustang fighter crashed after developing engine trouble. He was flying his 205th operation. (Richard E. Flagg)

Stansted Mountfitchet collided in bad weather over Theydon Mount, Epping, killing all twelve airmen. It was the crews' third mission since arriving at their new airfield.

Accidents continued to occur. Just a week later, a brand-new B-17 of the 381st Bombardment Group crashed shortly after take-off from Ridgewell. Mechanical problems were blamed for the accident, which claimed the lives of ten men – most of whom were flying their first mission. In 1998, a plaque listing the names of those killed was placed in St Augustine's Church, Birdbrook, close to where the bomber had crashed.

To the memory of
**the crew of the USAF BI7 Flying Fortress from the 381st Bomb Group
based at Ridgewell, which crashed in this parish at 05.50hrs March 24th 1944**

HEROES ALL

Pilot	2nd Lt. Kenneth T. Haynes. Florida	Radio Operator	S/Sgt. Edward C. Sauld. Wisconsin
Co-pilot	2nd Lt. Ralph P. Bemis. Kansas	Gunner	Sgt. Kenneth M. Ham. Kansas
Navigator	2nd Lt. Edmond P. Cusson. Massachusetts	Gunner	Sgt. Zeke P. Herrera. Texas
Bombardier	2nd Lt. Harry J. Stahlecker. New York	Gunner	Sgt. Donald B. Mahaffey. California
Engineer	S/Sgt. Harry L. Loparco. New York	Gunner	Sgt. Arthur M. Plows. Michigan

Another memorial to a tragedy. This tablet was unveiled in Birdbrook's St Augustine's Church to remember the men of a B-17 from RAF Ridgewell, which crashed close by on 24 March 1944. (Richard E. Flagg)

On 11 April 1944, Commander-in-Chief of the Allied Expeditionary Forces General Dwight D. Eisenhower chose RAF Great Dunmow as the first airfield to visit on his tour of American bases in England. Standing on the balcony of its control tower, Eisenhower watched thirty-nine of the 386th Bombardment Group's B-26s take-off to attack rail yards in Belgium. Two days later, Eisenhower formally assumed direction of all air operations out of the United Kingdom. The 386th was duly selected to drop the final wave of bombs on German gun positions before the Normandy beach landings began.

Alongside 'softening-up' raids on German positions near the French coastline, the RAF continued to bomb German cities. On 25 April 1944, 637 British bombers attacked Karlsruhe. On their return, an Avro Lancaster of No. 626 Squadron from RAF Wickenby in Lincolnshire came under attack by a lone Luftwaffe intruder. With a wing on fire, the pilot attempted to make an emergency landing at Boxted. Descending through thick fog, the Lancaster crashed into the edge of the airfield, killing all seven men onboard. In 2013, a memorial to the event was unveiled in Colchester.

Poor weather conditions finally brought American aircraft to the new airfield at Birch on 13 May, when four Lockheed P-38 Lightnings were forced to land on their return to RAF Warmwell in Dorset. Despite obstructions placed along the length of Birch's runway, all four landed safely. One of sixty-six planned 8th and 9th Air Force stations in Great Britain then operational, Birch would never again be used by the Americans. It would remain largely dormant until the RAF arrived in March 1945.

Nevertheless, the steadfast cooperation between the Americans and British continued in the lead-up to D-Day. By now, the Allied air forces were flying up to 4,000 sorties in a 'dawn to dusk' offensive against targets in Europe.

On 27 May 1944, over 1,100 American bombers and 700 fighters were despatched to France and Germany. Shortly after take-off from Little Walden, an A-20 Havoc collided

Unveiled on 25 April 2013, this square plinth and tablet records the seven names of a Lancaster bomber crew from RAF Wickenby whose aircraft crashed in Colchester on 25 April 1944. (Richard E. Flagg)

An aerial view of the former RAF Birch. Allocated to, but never used by, the 8th Air Force, it was primarily employed as a reserve transport airfield before finally being closed in 1945. (Richard E. Flagg)

with a low-flying P-51 operating from Fowlmere, Cambridgeshire. Both aircraft came down on Puddle Wharf Farm, Ashdon. Farmer's widow Elizabeth Everitt, who had been out walking her dog, witnessed the accident. She immediately rushed to the site of the burning A-20 and managed to rescue one of its crew members, before returning to extricate another. Suddenly, the aircraft exploded, killing her and its remaining three crew members. Elizabeth Everitt was posthumously awarded the Albert Medal (now replaced by the George Cross) and her name was added to the parish war memorial in All Saints Church, Ashdon. An announcement of her Albert Medal award was also made in the *London Gazette*:

> The King has been pleased to approve that the Albert Medal be awarded posthumously to Mrs. Elizabeth Ann Everitt, in recognition of the conspicuous gallantry which she displayed in her efforts to rescue the crew of a burning aircraft which crashed, loaded with bombs, into a field near her home. Two of the bombs subsequently exploded, killing her instantly.

Ten days after Elizabeth Everitt's death, eight B-26 groups, three A-20 units and a single B-17 formation took off from Essex to attack positions on the Normandy coastline. At the same time, P-51s, P-47s and P-38s departed from three other Essex bases to escort the bombers and an armada of vessels streaming towards France. The RAF also despatched its Mosquitoes and Spitfires from Bradwell Bay for offensive and defensive duties. All but the

In commemoration of **ELIZABETH EVERITT'S** bravery when she lost her life in attempting the rescue of an American airman from a burning aeroplane at Ashdon, on 27. May 1944, a sum of £180 was collected and presented to Saffron Walden Hospital

One of only sixteen women to be awarded the Albert Medal for gallantry, Elizabeth Everitt's sacrifice during the rescue of American airmen is still remembered in her home village today. (Richard E. Flagg)

B-17s were daubed with black and white 'invasion stripes'. A total of 14,674 sorties were flown by the Allied air forces during the first twenty-four hours of 6 June 1944. In contrast, the Luftwaffe flew a mere 319 operations.

With the British people believing themselves safe after the start of the Allied invasion, the Germans turned to another weapon in response. The first Vergeltungswaffen-1 ('vengeance weapon-1', or V-1) – a pilotless aircraft fitted with a bomb – landed in London just six days after D-Day. Three days later, the first V-1 fell on Essex. By the end of June, seventeen had reached East Anglia, most of which had fallen on the county. By July, an average of 100 V-1s were landing in England every day.

In response, the Allied air forces were tasked with destroying the launch sites in northern France. On 19 June, the 379th Bombardment Group despatched its B-17s to bomb a position at Zudausques. On their return, just as they were descending through clouds over the Thames Estuary, two of the Flying Fortresses collided. Six crew members managed to bail out of one, which nose-dived into the north bank of the Thames, near Canvey Island. The other came to rest just below the water's surface in a mine field, where it was left to remain undisturbed. A total of eleven crewmen were listed as missing or killed. A plaque was later unveiled at Paddocks Garden on Canvey Island to commemorate the event, while a further addition saw an information board erected on 19 June 2015 – exactly seventy-one years after the event.

The Normandy landings soon allowed Allied troops to capture French airfields previously used by the Luftwaffe. In line with its doctrine that 'mobility on the ground is what flexibility is in the air', the 9th Air Force began moving many of its bomber groups closer to the south coast of England in preparation for a crossing of the Channel. On 18 July, Chipping Ongar saw the departure of its B-26s to Hampshire, while Earls Colne

Unveiled in November 1996, this plaque in Paddocks Garden, Canvey Island, remembers the crews of two B-17s from RAF Kimbolton that collided in 1944. In 2015, a local playing field was renamed 'B17 Memorial Ground'. (Richard E. Flagg)

witnessed the final mission of the 323rd Bombardment Group carried out from Essex. Six days later, the B-26s of the 394th Bombardment Group left Boreham for their 'advanced landing ground' in the New Forest.

Rivenhall was the next to bid farewell to the Americans when the 397th Bombardment Group left for its new base in Hampshire on 5 August. Nevertheless, Essex's residents continued to see the county's only heavy bombers on an almost daily basis.

On 5 August, the 381st Bombardment Group's B-17s left Ridgewell to attack a major German rocket development site at Peenemünde on the Baltic coast. Shortly after take-off, an aircraft nicknamed *Dry Gulcher* caught fire. Her co-pilot, Captain Irving Moore, attempted to keep the B-17 level but soon realised he was losing control. Most of the crew immediately bailed out but the tail gunner, Harold Norris, was unable to escape from his position. *Dry Gulcher* came down in a field behind Shalford church and exploded, killing Norris. Remarkably, despite extensive damage to a number of surrounding buildings, no one on the ground was injured. In June 2008 a memorial was erected close to the site and lists the names of the crew. In later life, Irving Moore went on to direct the 1980s TV series *Dallas*, including the now-famous 'Who shot J.R.?' episode.

Ridgewell had already played host to celebrity visits by James Cagney, Vivien Leigh, Laurence Olivier and Edward G. Robinson when world-famous American singer and movie star Bing Crosby arrived at the airfield on 2 September 1944. For two hours he entertained an estimated 4,000 people in one of its two hangars before moving on to Suffolk.

By now, Gosfield, Matching and Wethersfield had seen the departure of their American bomb groups for reconstructed airfields in northern France. Britain had also experienced the first of some 9,000 Vergeltungswaffen-2 (V-2 rockets) launched against it. Capable of

A fine memorial located in the village of Shalford remembers the crash of a B-17. One airman was killed, while nine others bailed out, including Irving Moore – director of the 1980s TV series *Dallas*. (Richard E. Flagg)

reaching 70 miles (113 km) into the stratosphere before falling back to Earth at 4,000 mph (6,437 km/h), the V-2 arrived too fast to be seen or heard. Nevertheless, to allay fears, the British government began encouraging rumours that gas mains were exploding.

The residents of Greensted Juxta Ongar could have been forgiven for thinking one had blown up on 23 September when a massive explosion shook the ground near St Andrew's Church. The incident involved neither a gas main nor a V-2, but an RAF Avro Lancaster of No. 582 (Pathfinder) Squadron from Little Staughton, Cambridgeshire. During a fighter affiliation exercise, the aircraft went out of control before crashing into the ground, killing all seven men onboard. In common with other aircraft crash sites close to Essex churches, a memorial plaque was placed in St Andrew's to honour the crew.

The next day, an American B-26 Marauder, nicknamed *Lilly Commando*, was returning to Matching from its new base in Amy, France, when it encountered severe weather conditions over Essex. Battling strong winds, the aircraft ran out of fuel. It was thought that the pilot, Second Lieutenant Jack T. Hanlon, was attempting to ditch in water near Ashingdon. Unfortunately, the 'water' turned out to be a flooded field. The B-26 crashed on landing, killing all four men onboard. A brass plaque was unveiled by the 1st Ashingdon (St Andrew's) Scout Group in Ashingdon Church Hall in 2009, its epitaph simply reading: 'VIRTUTE ALISQUE – With Wings and Courage'.

Andrews Field was the next Essex airfield to see the Americans leave, when its resident 322nd Bombardment Group departed for Beauvais, France. Little Walden then saw a

Fixed to the wall of Greensted Juxta Ongar's St Andrew's Church (reputedly the world's oldest surviving wooden church) is a plaque remembering the crew of a Lancaster that crashed near the village during a training sortie in 1944. (Richard E. Flagg)

Dedicated to the crew of
B26 B 42-96102

Lilly Commando

Along with the crews of Baby Doll and Miss Laid
'The Marauder Men'

Who lost their lives so far away from home
24th September 1944

2nd Lt. Jack T. Hanlon
1st Lt. Jay M. Sink Jr.
SSgt. William L. McCarty
Cpl. Gerald F. Smith

VIRTUTE ALISQUE - With Wings and Courage

1st Ashingdon (St. Andrew's) Scout Group

Another plaque to commemorate another accident – this time the crash of B-26 *Lilly Commando*, a Marauder that went down near Ashingdon in 1944. The plaque was unveiled by a local Scout group in 2009. (Richard E. Flagg)

change in ownership when the 409th Bombardment Group was replaced by the 361st Fighter Group. Its P-51 Mustangs immediately went into action over Kassel, Germany, in support of the 445th Bombardment Group's B-24 Liberators. The 445th subsequently lost twenty-five bombers in arguably the most concentrated air battle of the Second World War. Only four B-24s managed to return safely to their base in Norfolk. Nevertheless, the 361st had prevented the 445th's complete annihilation by accounting for eighteen German fighters – the highest tally for any fighter group engaged in a single day's combat.

Andrews Field, Earls Colne and Wethersfield were all handed back to the RAF on 1 October 1944, while Great Dunmow waved off the last of Essex's B-26 bombers a day later. RAF Mustangs then arrived at Andrews Field, which would eventually house the largest number of British P-51s operating from a single airfield.

On the day that Andrews Field was transferred to the RAF, a P-47 Thunderbolt of the 78th Fighter Group based at Duxford, Cambridgeshire, was involved in a mid-air collision with a B-17 over Greenstead Green, 11 miles east of Great Saling. Although the B-17 sustained damage, it returned safely to its base at Snetterton Heath. The P-47, on the other hand, crashed straight down into a field close to St James's Church, Greenstead Green. Again, a plaque was later unveiled in honour of its pilot, Second Lieutenant Dwight G. Belt, who lost his life.

Rivenhall saw the arrival of RAF No. 295 Squadron on 11 October, which brought Short Stirlings back to Essex. Another two squadrons of Stirlings then arrived at Great Dunmow to take part in 'Special Duties'. Three weeks later, No. 295 Squadron despatched eight

Unveiled in 1978, this plaque in Greenstead Green Church honours Second Lieutenant Dwight G. Belt, whose P-47 crashed nearby after colliding with a B-17 on 1 October 1944. (Richard E. Flagg)

of its bombers to Norway for a Special Operations Executive drop. Yet, it was a Stirling from No. 190 Squadron at Great Dunmow that became the first casualty of these new clandestine operations.

On 21 November, a Stirling pilot was being checked on a night glider-towing sortie. After successfully releasing the glider, the bomber circled Great Dunmow before clipping some trees, skidding into a field and striking a bank of earth. The aircraft exploded, killing its crew of seven. Despite a subsequent enquiry that found the pilot, Flying Officer J. I. Kidgell, had failed to monitor his instruments, it has since been asserted that the Stirling was actually shot down by a German night fighter that was seen to be following it. A memorial plaque to the incident was later unveiled in the grounds of Easton Lodge, Little Easton.

On 19 December, the British government finally released details of the V-2 rockets that had been regularly falling on the country. Part of the announcement stated: 'The rumbling sound, like thunder, after the explosion, is the noise of the passage of the rocket through the air. It is not heard until after the explosion as the rocket is travelling so much faster than sound.'

A plaque in the grounds of Easton Lodge now remembers the crew of an RAF Short Stirling that crashed after releasing a Horsa glider over Great Dunmow on 21 November 1944. (Richard E. Flagg)

Earlier that morning, workers at the Hoffmann Manufacturing Company in Chelmsford – Britain's first ball bearing factory – failed to hear the V-2 that struck their plant. Thirty-nine people were killed and 138 injured, forty-seven seriously. A memorial service was held at Chelmsford Cathedral exactly one year later, while a plaque was also unveiled at the factory itself. Today, only the individual graves of those who lost their lives serve as reminders of Essex's deadliest V-2 attack.

Ardleigh had been struck by a V-1 three months earlier, which killed four people. Yet, twelve days after the Hoffmann incident, a huge explosion took place at Wick Farm, 2 miles west of the village. Lieutenant Samuel K. Batson of the 56th Fighter Group had taken off from nearby Boxted in a P-47 originally flown by the group's famed commander, Major Hubert 'Hub' Zemke. Suffering engine failure shortly afterwards, the aircraft crashed, killing Batson. He is now remembered on the Millennium Green war memorial in Ardleigh, while a replica P-47 (sporting the same markings and serial number) is on display in the American Air Museum at Duxford's Imperial War Museum.

At the time of Batson's crash, 'Hub' Zemke had transferred to the 479th Fighter Group at RAF Wattisham, Suffolk. The 479th was the last fighter group to join the 8th Air Force, arriving in England in May 1944. On 13 January 1945, Zemke's group escorted a formation of heavy bombers to Germany. On their return to Wattisham, a P-51 nicknamed *Little Zippie*, flown by Flight Officer Raymond E. King, suffered mechanical problems and crashed into the sea close to Clacton. King was rescued unconscious but died shortly after

A replica of Republic P-47D Thunderbolt 42-26413 *Oregon's Britannia*, on display in the American Air Museum, Duxford. Originally assigned to Major Hubert Zemke, the aircraft later crashed while being piloted by Lieutenant Samuel K. Batson. (Authors' Collection)

Unveiled on the fiftieth anniversary of his death in 1995, this memorial at Albany Gardens remembers Flight Officer Raymond E. King, whose P-51 crashed into the sea off Clacton in January 1945. (Richard E. Flagg)

being brought ashore. His P-51 was recovered by members of the East Essex Aviation Society in 1987 and is now on display in its museum. In 1995, a memorial was also erected in memory of Raymond E. King, which now stands in Albany Gardens, Clacton.

Accidents had become commonplace. Five weeks after King's death another P-51, belonging to the 55th Fighter Group at Wormingford, crashed close to North Stifford during high-altitude formation training. Although the cause of the crash was never determined, its pilot, Lieutenant Samuel E. Kershaw, was killed. In 1999, a stone tablet was unveiled in Kershaw's memory and a road in Chafford Hundred named Kershaw Close.

On 28 February 1945, Andrews Field welcomed the arrival of Britain's first jet fighter, the Gloster Meteor. No. 616 Squadron – the first unit to receive the jet – used the Essex airfield for a month before moving on to the Netherlands.

Five days after No. 616 Squadron arrived at Andrews Field, 760 British aircraft were in action over Chemnitz, Germany. No. 432 (Royal Canadian Air Force) Squadron's Halifax bombers lifted off from East Moor, Yorkshire, to take part in the raid, which was carried out successfully. However, on their return to England, one aircraft was shot down by British anti-aircraft guns positioned at Walton-on-the-Naze. All eight Canadian crewmen were killed. In 1978, a memorial, fashioned from the aircraft's recovered propeller blades, was unveiled in memory of the crew.

By mid-March, Essex's airfields began witnessing the arrival of huge numbers of RAF bombers, transporters and gliders. They were joined by thousands of troops from the British 6th Airborne Division. All had arrived in Essex to take part in Operation Varsity – an airborne assault on German positions on the River Rhine, designed to allow Allied ground troops to enter northern Germany. An estimated 500 aircraft took off from Birch,

The village of North Stifford witnessed the crash of an American P-51 fighter on 21 February 1945. Its pilot, Second Lieutenant Samuel E. Kershaw, is remembered in the name of Kershaw Close, Chafford Hundred. (Richard E. Flagg)

This stone pillar, complete with recovered propeller blades, was dedicated in 1979 to remember the crew of a Halifax bomber that crashed in March 1945 while returning from a bombing operation. (Richard E. Flagg)

Boreham, Chipping Ongar, Earls Colne, Gosfield, Matching, Rivenhall and Wethersfield on 24 March, carrying troops, jeeps, trailers and equipment necessary for the assault. The operation, which was eventually coined 'Little D-Day' by British newspapers, became the largest airborne operation ever conducted in one day on a single location.

On 25 April 1945, the last remaining American units in Essex carried out their final combat missions. Twelve days later, the German High Command signed the unconditional surrender of all German forces. 'Victory in Europe' Day (VE Day) was celebrated twenty-four hours later. The commander of the 8th Air Force, General James 'Jimmy' Doolittle, then authorised his ground crews to begin making aerial tours of Germany 'to see with their own eyes what they had helped to bring about'.

Two days later, a formation of B-17s from the 379th Bombardment Group took off from Kimbolton on a German 'sightseeing' tour. Overflying Braintree on the morning of 10 May, one of the B-17s encountered turbulence and lost control. It lurched down on top of another, slicing it in two and sending it crashing down into a field near Bocking. Eleven men were killed just two days after the war had ended. Seventy years to the day of the accident, a memorial was unveiled close to the site where the bomber crashed. It is yet another field of America.

Above: On 24 March 1945, the largest airborne operation in history got underway. Several Essex airfields witnessed the departure of bombers towing gliders that were taking part in Operation Varsity. (Authors' Collection)

Left: Seventy years to the day, this information board was unveiled in Braintree to remember the crash of a B-17 near the town. The accident took place just forty-eight hours after VE Day. (Richard E. Flagg)

CHAPTER FIVE

Lasting Legacies

To those who survive I would say this, content yourself and take credit with those who perished that now the "Cease Fire" has sounded countless homes within our Empire will welcome back a father, husband or son whose life, but for your endeavours and your sacrifices, would assuredly have been expended during long further years of agony... Famously have you fought. Well have you deserved of your country and her Allies.

> Arthur Harris, Commander-in-Chief, RAF Bomber Command, 16 May 1945

Within months of VE Day, many of Essex's twenty-three wartime airfields lay idle. Some, like Stansted Mountfitchet and Rivenhall, were used to house prisoners of war or 'travellers of the road'. Others, like Debden and Ridgewell, quickly became RAF training centres and bomb storage depots. Many, however, were placed into 'care and maintenance' or broken up.

In salute to those who had fought during the Battle of Britain, a formation of 300 aircraft carried out a 'Victory Flypast' over London on 15 September. Taking off from North Weald,

A formation of twelve Lancaster bombers overfly London's Trafalgar Square in celebration of Victory in Europe. (Authors' Collection)

the parade was organised and led by the legendary fighter pilot Douglas Bader – North Weald fighter sector's new commander, who had been released from Colditz Castle earlier that year.

Just over a year later, Stansted Mountfitchet was opened for civilian use. London Aero & Motor Services Ltd arrived at the airfield on 15 December 1946 with three ex-RAF Halifaxes, which were subsequently used for cargo charter flights. A few weeks later, civil flying resumed at Rochford, which had become known as Southend Municipal Airport. By 1951, construction had begun on a new terminal building.

RAF Wethersfield, which had suffered construction delays during the Second World War, found itself in line for reconstruction when the RAF handed the airfield to the newly independent United States Air Force (USAF). Heightened tensions with the Soviet Union had seen the Americans begin to re-establish a presence in the UK. Plans were quickly drawn up for a major expansion of wartime airfields to accommodate the new jet aircraft then in service. On 24 August 1951, Wethersfield was assigned to the 3rd Air Force of the USAF. Nine months later, the 20th Fighter-Bomber Wing arrived from Virginia, USA, at a renovated Wethersfield with three squadrons of Republic F-84 Thunderjets.

Fast military jets soon became a common sight over Essex. On 10 September 1951, a Gloster Meteor from RAF No. 263 Squadron, at Wattisham, was overflying Southend-on-Sea when it broke up in mid-air and crashed over a wide area. Three people were killed on the ground by falling debris, while the pilot, Lionel Millikin, was later found strapped in his seat. He too was dead. A story then circulated that he had been performing a 'victory roll' in honour of a female acquaintance who was teaching at a nearby primary school.

Southend Municipal Airport's terminal building and forecourt, pictured sometime during the 1960s. (Authors' Collection)

A nuclear-capable F-84 Thunderstreak of the 20th Fighter-Bomber Wing at RAF Wethersfield. Wethersfield was the last of Essex's airfields to host American military aircraft. (Peter Bell)

No. 72 Squadron – another Gloster Meteor unit, based at RAF Odiham, Hampshire – had been reformed in 1947, having been a Spitfire squadron during the Second World War. Just over a year after Millikin's accident, two of the squadron's Meteors were hurtling over Essex when they collided above the village of Great Totham, killing both pilots and injuring two people on the ground. The village sign has since become the location for a plaque commemorating the tragic event.

In 1954, the Americans returned to Stansted Mountfitchet to begin construction work on its main wartime runway. It was duly extended to 10,000 feet (3,050 metres) in preparation for a possible transfer to the US Strategic Air Command as a rotational base for its new heavy bombers. Nevertheless, the possibility never became a reality and the airfield remained in civilian use.

Hidden on Great Totham's village sign, this plaque records the collision of two Gloster Meteors over the village in 1952. The village green became the base for recovery operations. (Richard E. Flagg)

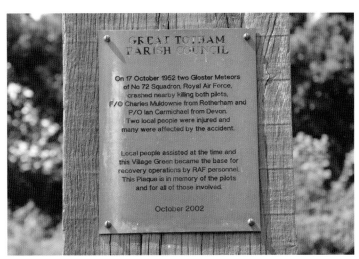

By then, North American F-100 Super Sabres had arrived at RAF Wethersfield. One accident had already claimed the life of a USAF pilot close to Sible Hedingham, in 1957, when a second crash occurred six years later.

During a routine instrument-navigation flight on 15 January 1963, Colonel Wendell J. Kelley, a Second World War and Korea veteran, was flying as part of a two-man crew. Shortly after take-off, smoke began to fill the cockpit. With the aircraft losing power and external fuel tanks slowing the aircraft down, the crew were directed over the North Sea, where the tanks were jettisoned. Returning to Wethersfield in poor weather conditions, the aircraft suffered further mechanical problems. Kelley instructed the pilot, First Lieutenant Paul M. Briggs, to 'blow the canopy', which he did. Briggs successfully ejected before the F-100 crashed next to the village of Gosfield. It is believed that Kelley had remained in the aircraft after spotting a built-up area below and attempted to steer it away. His body was found a few yards from the main wreckage shortly after the crash. Some years later, a memorial plaque was unveiled in a local playing field in memory of Colonel Kelley.

In April 1966, the British Airports Authority (BAA) took over control of Stansted Mountfitchet from the Ministry of Aviation. Numerous legal arguments then followed after it was announced that the site was being held in reserve as a third London airport. A resultant government commission subsequently shortlisted four sites, none of which included the Essex airfield. By 1979, however, a government white paper on airport policy proposed long-term development of either Stansted or five other sites, including the former wartime airfield at Chipping Ongar (then known as Willingale). A year later, the BAA submitted its own planning application to the local district council to develop Stansted. Future plans included the construction a new terminal alongside the existing runway, and the safeguarding of land to enable the addition of a second runway.

After a 258-day public enquiry, the British government granted approval for the phased development of Stansted's airfield and terminal. The permission allowed the airport to work to a capacity of 15 million passengers a year, with a cap on the numbers of aircraft

In memory of Colonel Wendell J. Kelly, a group of trees were planted in Gosfield's playing field. It is believed that Kelly had steered his stricken F-100 away from a nearby primary school. (Richard E. Flagg)

operating. Nevertheless, the proposed second runway was rejected. By 1986, work began on the new Stansted Airport.

Essex's other international airport, Southend, was soon lagging behind Stansted. Between the 1960s and 1970s, it had been the busiest of the two, breaking a record in 1967 when 692,686 passengers took off from its runways. A decline in scheduled flights through the 1970s then saw the airport evolve into an engineering and maintenance base. It came at a time when the town of Southend held its first public air display in 1986, becoming Europe's largest free air show for the next twenty-seven years.

Southend Airport was particularly active at night, especially with cargo flights. Just after 3:30 a.m. on 12 September 1987, a Beechcraft Super King Air of National Airways took off for Bergamo, Italy, carrying a full load of magazines and newspapers. A few minutes later, the aircraft crashed onto an empty car showroom near Rayleigh. A huge fire then followed, causing 200 people to be evacuated from their homes. It was believed that the pilot, New Zealander Hugh Forrester-Brown, had been attempting to force-land on Eastwood Road, but had steered his aircraft away from houses before crashing. Sometime later, a plaque was unveiled in his memory at the site of the accident.

When construction work on Stansted's new terminal building commenced in 1988, the Cold War was ending. This, combined with budget cutbacks and the growth of London's third international airport, compelled the USAF to leave RAF Wethersfield after twenty-seven years. Although service families from USAF bases at Alconbury, Molesworth and Upwood continued to use its military housing area, Wethersfield was handed back to the RAF on 3 July 1990.

Eight months later, on 15 March 1991, Queen Elizabeth II officially opened Stansted's new £400 million terminal building. Four days later, the first flight took off for Glasgow. The arrival of several low-cost carriers in 1997 then saw a huge spike in aircraft movements and passenger numbers. With Stansted close to exceeding its permitted capacity, the BAA made another application to Uttlesford District Council to increase the permitted number of movements and remove the cap on passenger numbers. Despite

Another tragedy thought to have happened after a pilot steered his aircraft away from a built-up area, this plaque remembers New Zealander Hugh Forrester-Brown, killed at Rayleigh in 1987. (Richard E. Flagg)

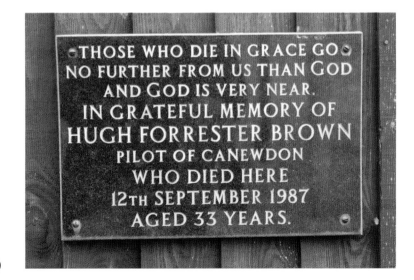

•THOSE WHO DIE IN GRACE GO•
NO FURTHER FROM US THAN GOD
AND GOD IS VERY NEAR.
IN GRATEFUL MEMORY OF
HUGH FORRESTER BROWN
PILOT OF CANEWDON
WHO DIED HERE
12TH SEPTEMBER 1987
AGED 33 YEARS.

The Queen opened Stansted's new terminal building and station on 15 March 1991. Since then, more than a quarter of a billion passengers have passed through its doors. (Authors' Collection)

a rejection and subsequent public enquiry, the BAA moved ahead with plans to extend its terminal building. The company was also keen to expand the airport as a whole and applied to increase its size by 3 square miles (8 square kilometres) and construct a second runway. Legal challenges and protests by environmental activists forced the BAA to subsequently withdraw its plans. Meanwhile, Southend Airport was undergoing something of a renaissance.

On 12 December 2008, the lease for the airport was sold to the Stobart Group at a cost of £21 million. A year later, the company made a planning application to extend its runway by 984 feet (300 metres). Construction work then began on the airport's new railway station, control tower and terminal building. Southend's resurgence was bolstered by an agreement which saw the low-cost carrier easyJet commit to seventy flights per week. On 5 March 2012, the new-look Southend Airport was officially unveiled.

Stansted, though, was not without its problems. In August 2012 – having been legally ordered by the Competition Commission to sell one of its airports – the BAA relented and agreed to sell Stansted. The following year, Manchester Airport Group (MAG), the owner of East Midlands and Bournemouth airports, bought Stansted for £1.5 billion. MAG subsequently announced that an £80 million redevelopment of the terminal building would take place (configured entirely for departures) and that a new arrivals terminal would also be built at a cost of £150 million. Part of an overall investment of £600 million, it followed a year in which Stansted processed 28 million passengers – a far cry from its birth as a wartime American bomber base.

With Stansted now the UK's fourth busiest airport and Southend ranked the best 'London' terminal by *Which?* magazine, the two Essex airports have survived many turbulent times. While the rest of the county's Second World War airfields have mostly reverted to agriculture, only a handful have retained any form of aviation. Andrewsfield,

London Southend Airport's new terminal building is fronted by *Searchlight Beacons* – a sculpture by John Atkin. It highlights the site's strategic importance throughout both world wars. (Authors' Collection)

Andrewsfield has hosted civil flying since 1972. Although most of its original buildings have long since gone, its American connection is still celebrated in murals and images hanging on its clubhouse walls. (Richard E. Flagg)

Another licenced airfield, Earls Colne's Anglian Flight Centre now offers training for Private Pilots' Licences using a fleet of Robin HR200 and Cessna 172 light aircraft. (Richard E. Flagg)

North Weald remains one of the best aviation facilities in Essex. The first International Air Tattoo was held here in 1971. It was also used as a backdrop for the TV production *Band of Brothers*. (Richard E. Flagg)

The Stapleford Flight Centre has been offering pilot training courses since 1953. With a fleet of over forty aircraft, it also offers London sightseeing flights and aircraft engineering services. (Richard E. Flagg)

Ridgewell is now home to the Essex Gliding Club, which uses a grassy segment of this former heavy bomber base close to the former perimeter track. Two of its gliders currently sport USAAF insignia. (Richard E. Flagg)

Wethersfield's main runway, showing little sign of wear and tear. The airfield was still being used for aviation until 2017, having hosted the RAF's No. 614 Volunteer Gliding Squadron since 1982. (Richard E. Flagg)

A small section of Wormingford's main runway has survived the passage of time and is now used by the Essex & Suffolk Gliding Club. (Richard E. Flagg)

Earls Colne, North Weald and Stapleford all remain active airfields today, while Ridgewell, Wethersfield and Wormingford host glider activities.

Essex's First World War airfields have largely vanished altogether. While Southend Airport (formerly RFC Rochford) has survived and flourished, others reverted to agriculture even before the outbreak of the Second World War. Today, only one exists in its near-original state.

Stow Maries is Europe's largest surviving First World War aerodrome. Over a century after it was first established, the site is now being preserved thanks to a £1.5 million grant from the British government. Today, it boasts two grass runways, a temporary hangar (housing many British and German First World War aircraft) and a number of original buildings – including its airmen's mess and pilots' ready room. The museum also offers an insight into life on an RFC aerodrome tasked with the defence of London.

An image of a Wing aerial sports competition held at Stow Maries – an Essex aerodrome that had been built in 1916 to protect the capital and Home Front from German aerial bombardment. (Stow Maries Great War Aerodrome)

An aerial view of Stow Maries taken in 2015. Its twenty-four Grade II listed buildings now form the site for a museum, making it Europe's largest surviving First World War aerodrome. (Richard E. Flagg)

Housing grass runways, hangars (for aircraft conservation) and a pilots' ready room, Stow Maries offers a fascinating insight into life on a First World War aerodrome. (Richard E. Flagg)

Thanks to Stow Maries' volunteers and those at other aviation museums who continue to commemorate the history of Essex's airfields, the county's aviation heritage is being preserved for future generations. Yet, there are numerous monuments across Essex's 1,420 square miles that also tell a poignant tale of their own. Many are now hidden from view, but theirs are the stories we should never lose sight of.

The impressive brick-built memorial at the former RAF Boxted pays tribute to the units that used the airfield during its four-year operational lifespan. (Richard E. Flagg)

Opened in 1954, the Anglo-American Memorial Playing Field in Saffron Walden contains a monument of twenty-six plaques listing the names of those who lost their lives between 1939 and 1945. (Richard E. Flagg)

Timed to coincide with commemorations for the seventy-fifth anniversary of the Battle of Britain, RAF Debden's memorial was unveiled on 19 September 2015. It backs on to Debden's north–south runway, which stretches into the distance. (Richard E. Flagg)

The Airfields of Britain Conservation Trust (ABCT) was established 'to advance the education of the public in the history of British airfields'. ABCT's Airfield Marker Programme saw a plaque placed at Widford's First World War landing ground. (Richard E. Flagg)

Avro Vulcan B2 XL426 at Southend Airport. Maintained in full ground working condition, the Vulcan Restoration Trust preserves the aircraft in tribute to those who flew and maintained the Vulcan during the Cold War. (Richard E. Flagg)

Boxted Airfield Museum contains the UK's largest collection of B-26 Marauder artefacts. It includes the rear section of *Mr. Shorty*, a B-26 that ended the war having completed ninety-six missions. It was broken up shortly after and found in a Cheshire scrapyard in 1974. (Richard E. Flagg)

Captain Henry Clifford Stroud is buried in St Andrew's Church, Rochford. His is one of scores of final resting places in Essex brought about by the combined perils of aviation and conflict. (Richard E. Flagg)

Essex Memorials

LOCATION	DESCRIPTION	LAT & LONG	DETAILS
Andrewsfield	Airfield	51.895936, 0.451707	Memorabilia in flying club.
Ardleigh	Village green	51.923443, 0.983812	Ardleigh war memorial.
Ashdon	All Saints' Church	52.049391, 0.304411	Plaque remembering Elizabeth Everitt.
Ashen	Church of St Augustine of Canterbury	52.051728, 0.546771	381st Bombardment Group memorial plaque.
Ashen	Foxes Road / The Street	52.050254, 0.548435	Village sign with B-17.
Ashingdon	Ashingdon and East Hawkwell Memorial Hall	51.607384, 0.691875	B-26 'The Marauder Men' memorial.
Audley End	Audley End House and Gardens	52.020134, 0.219392	Polish SOE memorial.
Birdbrook	Church of St Augustine of Canterbury	52.042505, 0.487288	381st Bombardment Group B-17 crash memorial.
Birdbrook	Church of St Augustine of Canterbury	52.042505, 0.487288	Eric George Kendall, RAF tribute.
Boreham	Cranham Road	51.786656, 0.522334	Boreham Airfield USAAF memorial.
Boreham	Holts Lane	51.778889, 0.532181	394th Bombardment Group (M) memorial.
Boreham	St Andrew's Church	51.757705, 0.543227	American flag and plaque.

LOCATION	DESCRIPTION	LAT & LONG	DETAILS
Boreham	Main Road	51.762782, 0.544657	Painting and plaque in village hall.
Boxted	Boxted Airfield Museum, Langham Lane	51.937241, 0.922832	Lt. Col. James H. Howard memorial plaque.
Boxted	Park Lane, Langham Moor	51.943012, 0.935525	Boxted Airfield memorial.
Bradfield	Parish Church of St. Lawrence	51.933815, 1.117789	Squadron Commander Edwin Harris Dunning, Royal Naval Air Service. Plaques and grave.
Bradwell-on-Sea	Trusses Road	51.731359, 0.898461	RAF Bradwell Bay war memorial.
Bradwell-on-Sea	Village Hall	51.723387, 0.899064	Two plaques remembering the flying units based at the nearby airfield.
Braintree	Braintree Community Centre and Essex American Hall	51.877479, 0.555157	Historic record. Plaques now at Wethersfield Museum.
Braintree	River Mead	51.887469, 0.558682	B-17G Flying Fortress crash memorial.
Braintree	Our Lady Queen of Peace, RC Church	51.878725, 0.554430	Local airfields memorial plaque.
Burnham-on-Crouch	Exact location unknown	51.6301689, 0.8320756	Airfields of Britain Conservation Trust (ABCT) marker plaque.
Burton End	The Ash Pub	51.890680, 0.225489	Memorabilia inside.
Canewdon	Lark Hill Road / Anchor Lane / Scotts Hall Road	51.615295, 0.737648	Village sign depicts a Chain Home radar mast (RDF).
Canvey Island	The Paddocks, Long Road	51.520128, 0.589820	B-17 (44-6133 and 42-97942) mid-air collision memorial.
Chafford Hundred	Kershaw Close	51.486984, 0.295311	Lt. Samuel E. Kershaw memorial.
Chelmsford	Chelmsford Cathedral	51.735188, 0.472160	American memorial window and military chapel.
Chelmsford	Chelmsford library	51.734419, 0.470213	Essex airfields in the Battle of Britain memorial plaque.
Chelmsford	Hall Street / Mildmay Road	51.729361, 0.474844	Marconi: The World's First Wireless Factory blue plaque.
Chelmsford	Train station	51.736679, 0.468841	Frederick Herbert Hunt 1920–1943 blue plaque.

LOCATION	DESCRIPTION	LAT & LONG	DETAILS
Chigwell	Manor Road	51.610462, 0.080925	Second World War air raid memorial.
Chingford	West Essex Golf Club	51.650026, 0.011269	Memorial bench remembering the servicemen at nearby Lippitts Hill anti-aircraft gun battery.
Clacton	Albany Gardens Marine Parade East	51.793571, 1.169567	Flt Off Raymond E. King memorial.
Clacton	Off Marine Parade West	51.782316, 1.144429	Sir Winston Churchill memorial.
Clacton	Seafront Gardens	51.786656, 1.152959	RAF & RAFA memorials.
Clacton	Victoria Road	51.794307, 1.164989	Memorial bench.
Clavering	Church of St Mary and St Clement	51.965325, 0.139557	Royal Australian Air Force memorial altar.
Colchester	A12 Ipswich Road	51.916610, 0.930992	Lancaster (DV177) crash memorial.
Colchester	Butt Road	51.885911, 0.894575	Plaque commemorating the first Colchester air raid.
Colchester	Chapel Street South	51.886574, 0.896832	Chapel Street air raid memorial plaque.
Colchester	Colchester Zoo	51.861956, 0.831513	210 Airmobile plaque.
Colchester	Merville Barracks	51.875603, 0.892508	Douglas DC-3 Dakota IV gate guard.
Colchester	St Johns Green	51.885793, 0.899983	Essex Anglo American Goodwill Association memorial.
Debden	Water Lane	51.985514, 0.277640	RAF and USAAF memorials.
Dedham	Parish Church	51.958577, 0.992761	A. H. Christey Memorial Pew with the RAF badge.
Earls Colne	Earls Colne Business Park	51.911689, 0.695150	Airfield memorial at entrance.
Eastwood	St Laurence and All Saints' Church	51.567724, 0.684920	Plaque remembering Sgt E. J. Coe, who was killed in an Avro Lancaster.
Epping	Cemetery	51.698968, 0.096773	Commonwealth War Graves Commission plot with numerous air force graves.
South Fambridge	Fambridge Road	51.629775, 0.677864	ABCT marker stone.
Fyfield	Village Hall, Houchin Drive	51.737035, 0.269354	ABCT marker plaque.

LOCATION	DESCRIPTION	LAT & LONG	DETAILS
Goldhangar	Gardeners Farm Shop, Maldon Road	51.739962, 0.736748	Memorial plaque on old aerodrome site.
Gosfield	Church of St Catherine	51.934715, 0.584590	B-26 model and memorial in the church.
Gosfield	Gosfield playing fields	51.937662, 0.589606	Col. Wendell J Kelly USAF memorial.
Gosfield	Maurice Rowson Hall, Church Road	51.935986, 0.588756	410th Bombardment Group memorial next to hall.
Grays	Gunning Road	51.480207, 0.338573	P/O Peter S. Gunning memorial.
Great Burstead	Church of St Mary Magdalene	51.603928, 0.425379	Zeppelin L32 crew burial register.
Great Dunmow	Stortford Road	51.872119, 0.354847	Sergeant Hugh Holt memorial bench.
Great Dunmow	Newton Green	51.873544, 0.353510	Flight Sergeant Reginald Matthew Dauncey memorial bench.
Great Dunmow	Primary school	51.873005, 0.349600	Flight Sergeant Arthur George Reid and Flight Sergeant Ronald David Payne memorial benches.
Great Dunmow	Woodlands Walk	51.875696, 0.348212	Flying Office William Walter D'Arcy Brain and Flying Officer James Ian Kidgell.
Great Dunmow	B1256 / Stortford Road	51.868434, 0.316068	Essex Anglo American Goodwill Association (EAAGA) / 386th Bomb Group memorial.
Great Dunmow	Exact location unknown	51.8722508, 0.3522311	Flying Officer Ernest Douglas Woods memorial bench.
Great Notley	Windermere Drive	51.859626, 0.532650	White Court Park American hospital memorial.
Great Saling	Blake End Road	51.893624, 0.471970	Andrewsfield Airfield memorial.
Great Saling	Vicarage Close	51.902548, 0.471681	819th Engineer Aviation Battalion memorial.
Great Totham	B1022 / Chapel Road Junction	51.784732, 0.706382	Plaque on Great Totham village sign.
Great Wigborough	St Stephen's Church	51.804817, 0.853342	Framed account of the shooting down of Zeppelin L33.
Great Yeldham	Ridgewell Airfield Commemorative Museum	52.027102, 0.546116	381st Bombardment Group memorial.

LOCATION	DESCRIPTION	LAT & LONG	DETAILS
Great Yeldham	Ridgewell Airfield Commemorative Museum	52.027210, 0.546102	RAF memorial.
Greenstead Green	Church of St James the Great	51.924882, 0.648678	Plaque in memory of 2nd Lt Dwight G. Belt, USAAF.
Greensted Juxta Ongar	Church of St Andrew	51.704401, 0.225479	Lancaster crash memorial plaque.
Hadstock	Bartlow Road	52.080252, 0.274354	Village sign with control tower.
Harold Park	A12 Colchester Road	51.603498, 0.247599	Plaque on house to William Blair Pattullo (private residence).
Hornchurch	Library in North Street	51.564912, 0.220440	Wall display in foyer relating to RAF Hornchurch, No. 122 Squadron and the Battle of Britain.
Hornchurch	St Andrews Church	51.560481, 0.226161	Stained glass window with Spitfire.
Hornchurch	South End Road	51.540636, 0.202720	The Good Intent pub had a Spitfire on the sign, although it is not known if it still exists.
Lambourne	St Mary and All Saints' Church	51.644229, 0.135695	Sub Lieutenant W. C. Lewis-Lavender RNVR memorial.
Leigh-on-Sea	Church of St Margaret	51.548544, 0.643845	Altar rails in memory of F/O Pusey and crew of Lancaster DS630.
Leigh-on-Sea	Church of St Margaret	51.548544, 0.643845	Sgt J. N. Boston (rear gunner) No. 640 Sqn stained glass window.
Lippitts Hill	Public footpath near Police Air Support Unit	51.655145, 0.015768	EAAGA memorial.
Little Easton	St Mary's Church	51.886954, 0.330115	Stained glass windows and memorial plaques.
Little Easton	Easton Lodge	51.893318, 0.315661	Gardens with memorial plaques.
Little Walden	B1052 (Little Walden Road)	52.050695, 0.253577	Village sign.
Little Walden	B1052 (Little Walden Road)	52.050647, 0.253497	War memorial mentions USAAF air base.
Little Walden	B1052 on Old Airfield	52.066710, 0.272059	Plaques in the control tower (now a private residence).

LOCATION	DESCRIPTION	LAT & LONG	DETAILS
Little Walden	Church of St John the Evangelist	52.049536, 0.253029	RAF Little Walden tapestry.
Little Wigborough	St Nicholas' Church	51.794435, 0.871208	Zeppelin L33 wreckage and memorabilia.
Little Yeldham	Church of St John the Baptist	52.025953, 0.591873	Sgt R. V. Smith (wireless operator) 30 OTU memorial plaque.
Loughton	Church of the Holy Innocents, High Beech	51.661680, 0.034406	Edmund Eric Horn, Royal Flying Corps memorial plaque.
Loughton	Clays Lane	51.661239, 0.067878	Everard Richard Calthrop, (Pioneer of the Parachute) blue plaque.
Loughton	Spareleaze Hill	51.646740, 0.064231	Rupert Arnold Brabner, DSO, DSC, MP, (1911–45), Commander, Fleet Air Arm blue plaque.
Lower Nazeing	Aerodrome Corner / Nazeing Road / B194	51.736973, -0.000886	Trees planted by the Royal British Legion and the Royal Air Force Association.
Magdalen Laver	Church of St Mary	51.752813, 0.190676	Flying Officer John Clarke Memorial Plaque.
Marks Hall	Arboretum	51.905916, 0.679305	Earls Colne airfield layout and memorial obelisk.
Matching	Anchor Lane	51.780090, 0.258123	391st Bombardment Group memorial.
Matching Green	Church of St Mary the Virgin	51.785579, 0.2100274	391st Bombardment Group memorial plaques.
Matching Green	Village Green	51.778019, 0.225021	Village sign with aircraft.
Moreton	Church of St Mary the Virgin	51.740994, 0.225359	P/O Goode (pilot) No. 114 Sqn memorial board.
Navestock	Church of St Thomas the Apostle	51.663087, 0.225878	Memorial rose garden.
Nazeing	Church of All Saints with St Giles	51.743633, 0.046323	Communal grave with celtic cross where ten villagers are buried as a result of enemy action in 1944.
North Weald	St Andrew's Church	51.725494, 0.163718	Memorabilia and CWGC plot.
North Weald	On a Second World War fighter pen on the airfield	51.721346, 0.150099	Nos 331 and 332 Squadrons Royal Norwegian Air Force memorial.

LOCATION	DESCRIPTION	LAT & LONG	DETAILS
North Weald	At the airfield	51.721159, 0.150997	Memorabilia and plaques at the Squadron Bar and Flying Club.
North Weald	Hampden Close	51.713719, 0.161677	Memorial to the nine soldiers from C Company, 7th Battalion, the Essex Regiment who lost their lives in an air raid.
North Weald	Hurricane Way	51.713108, 0.155728	North Weald airfield memorial.
North Weald	Epping Road / B181	51.712392, 0.154063	Officers' mess plaque.
North Weald	Hurricane Way	51.713332, 0.155712	Stained glass window at the Airfield Museum.
North Weald	At the airfield entrance	51.717479, 0.159378	The Spirit of North Weald gate guard.
North Weald	Wheelers Farm Gardens	51.716827, 0.167526	Village sign with Hurricane.
Orsett	Fire station	51.506639, 0.384494	Wg Cdr Reginald Grant memorial.
Orsett	Orsett Golf Club, Brentwood Road	51.501838, 0.390894	ABCT marker plaque.
Point Clear	Martello Tower at Pretoria Caravan Park	51.801052, 1.019772	Raymond E. King memorial.
Rayleigh	Sainsburys Local, Eastwood Road	51.578870, 0.620361	Hugh Forrester Brown memorial.
Ridgewell	Congregational Church	52.041559, 0.529794	Stained glass window.
Ridgewell	Church of St. Laurence	52.039258, 0.535287	American flag and plaque.
Ovington	Ashen Road	52.050030, 0.563079	Caroline memorial.
Rivenhall	Woodhouse Lane	51.849225, 0.656107	ABCT marker stone.
Rivenhall	Church Road / Oak Road	51.825245, 0.653149	Village sign.
Rivenhall End	Oak Road / Henry Dixon Road	51.818794, 0.664066	Village sign.
Rochford	Church of St Andrew	51.580321, 0.700186	War graves in the churchyard and propeller memorial inside the church.
Rochford	Old House, South Street	51.581312, 0.707281	Plaque in memory of Alan Walter Camp (RAFVR): 1920–1941.

LOCATION	DESCRIPTION	LAT & LONG	DETAILS
Roxwell	Church of St Michael and All Angels	51.750976, 0.382367	S/L D. M. Foreman DFC (pilot) No. 12 OTU memorial plaque.
Runwell	Runwell Community Primary School	51.622901, 0.524115	ABCT marker plaque.
Saffron Walden	Bridge End Gardens	52.027249, 0.237769	Anglo-American memorial.
Shalford	B1053 (Braintree Road) at entrance to church	51.933954, 0.505023	Boeing B-17 *Dry Gulcher* memorial
Shotgate	Hodgson Way	51.604632, 0.550331	P/O W. H. Hodgson memorial.
Silver End	Western Arms Pub, Western Road	51.843051, 0.631036	Rivenhall airfield memorial.
South Fambridge	Fambridge Road	51.629419, 0.677966	Village sign.
Southend	Airport	51.568994, 0.704166	Searchlight beacon.
Southend	Church of St John the Baptist	51.534045, 0.717019	F/L G. D. Body (pilot) No. 10 Sqn memorial plaque.
Southend	Church of St John the Baptist	51.534045, 0.717019	F/O R. B. Jennings (pilot) No. 18 OTU stained glass window.
Southend	Holy Trinity Church	51.541775, 0.741010	Sgt K. Merrifield (wireless operator) No. 61 Sqn memorial plaque.
Southend	Pier	51.533127, 0.715795	Red Arrows mosaic.
Southend	Shaftesbury Avenue	51.531754, 0.744771	Sgt Ian Clenshaw plaque (private residence).
Southend	Old passenger terminal at the airport	51.567785, 0.700153	RAF Rochford memorial plaque.
Stansted	First Avenue	51.882450, 0.216999	70th anniversary memorial plaque and tree.
Stansted	Airport terminal	51.889957, 0.261737	Memorial plaques and information boards in the terminal.
Stapleford Tawney	Airfield	51.656716, 0.156121	RAF Stapleford Tawney memorial.
Stock	All Saints' Church	51.661289, 0.438821	Plaque remembering wartime damage to church.
Stock	Our Lady and St Joseph Church	51.662071, 0.444013	Flight Lieutenant Reginald Eric Lovett DFC memorial.

LOCATION	DESCRIPTION	LAT & LONG	DETAILS
Stow Maries	Church of St Mary and St Margaret	51.663325, 0.649665	Plaques located in the church.
Stow Maries	The Street / Stow Road	51.665199, 0.649727	Village sign with aircraft.
Stow Maries	The Smythe Hall, Church Lane	51.664115, 0.649399	Propeller memorial plaque in village hall.
Stow Maries	Stow Maries Great War Aerodrome	51.669601, 0.629043	RFC memorial on the airfield.
Thaxted	Church of St John the Baptist	51.954289, 0.342029	Flight Sub Lieutenant C. R. W. Hodges, Royal Navy and family memorial plaque.
Thaxted	Public footpath near site of old landing ground	51.961779, 0.371734	ABCT marker plaque.
Ugley	Church of St Peter	51.936561, 0.209134	P/O W. F. Bunting DFM (navigator) No. 582 Sqn memorial.
Walthamstow	Walthamstow Marshes	51.567996, -0.051073	A. V. Roe plaque.
Walthamstow	Warner Estates – exact location unknown	n/a	2nd Lieutenant Harvey Dalton Johnson memorial.
Walton-on-the-Naze	B1336 (Walton Road)	51.848012, 1.267131	RAF, RAFA and Halifax (RG475) crash memorial.
West Horndon	Cadogan Avenue	51.571839, 0.345158	8th Air Force memorial bench.
Westcliff-on-Sea	St Saviour's Church	51.542168, 0.683210	R. W. Berry (rear gunner) No. 49 Sqn stained glass window.
Wethersfield	Shaw Drive	51.969250, 0.495672	Memorial plaques at the base chapel – permission to visit must be obtained.
Wickford	Dollymans Farm	51.594112, 0.558116	Memorial to Captain Alexander Bruce Kynoch of No. 37 Squadron Royal Flying Corps.
Wickford	Dollymans Farm	51.593925, 0.561754	Memorial to Captain Henry Clifford Stroud of No. 61 Squadron Royal Flying Corps.
Widford	Paradise Road	51.724489, 0.432785	ABCT marker plaque.
Willingale.	Church of St Andrew	51.741805, 0.310609	Plaques and memorabilia in church.
Willingale	The Street / Stow Road	51.742048, 0.310639	War memorial.

LOCATION	DESCRIPTION	LAT & LONG	DETAILS
Wormingford	Fordham Road	51.941365, 0.807345	362nd Fighter Group memorial.
Wormingford	Village hall	51.949352, 0.812153	Memorial plaques to the USAAF units based at Wormingford airfield.
Wormingford	Wormingford Airfield	51.944041, 0.803293	Memorial plaques and memorabilia at the Gliding Club.
Writtle	St Johns Green	51.732419, 0.431043	ABCT marker plaque.

Erected in 1920, this memorial to Captain Alexander Kynoch, killed in a collision over Shotgate in 1918, lies in a field close to the busy A130. It is one of Essex's oldest aviation monuments. (Paul Bingley)

Essex Airfields
(Civil, Military and Private)

Name 1	Name 2	Notes	AAF Sta.	Lat & Long	Opened	Closed
Abridge	Loughton			51.658000, 0.106028	1932	1939
Alphamstone	Clees Hall	Private strip		51.976908, 0.740978	Unknown	n/a
Andrews Field	Great Saling	USAAF	485	51.897222, 0.459094	1943	n/a
Ardleigh	Bounds Farm	Private strip		51.923936, 1.007892	Unknown	2017
Ardleigh	Blue Barns			51.930303, 0.950422	1931	1933
Ashingdon	Rochford			51.592372, 0.703117	1931	1935
Ashingdon	Canute Air Park			51.612389, 0.693278	1935	1936
Audley End		Private strip		52.007767, 0.224178	1983	n/a
Barking Creek	Creekmouth			51.516889, 0.112417	1909	1912
Barling	Baldwins Farm	Private strip		51.569664, 0.794675	Unknown	n/a
Beaumont					1916	1916
Belchamp Walter	Waits Farm	Private strip		52.033894, 0.638853	Unknown	n/a
Birch		USAAF	149	51.842328, 0.781736	1944	1945
Blackheath	Colchester			51.857639, 0.917694	1917	1920s
Boreham		USAAF	161	51.779278, 0.521328	1944	1945
Boreham		Police and Air Ambulance		51.781639, 0.521611	1989	2018
Boxted	Langham Moor	USAAF	150	51.935669, 0.930472	1943	1947
Boxted		Private strip		51.940750, 0.933222	Unknown	n/a

Name 1	Name 2	Notes	AAF Sta.	Lat & Long	Opened	Closed
Bradwell Bay		RAF		51.735739, 0.901544	1941	1946
Braintree	Boones Farm			51.912300, 0.590378	Unknown	Unknown
Braintree					1918	1918
Broomfield	Broomfield Court			51.774250, 0.453417	1916	1932
Broxbourne	Nazeing			51.739847, 0.003100	1930	1954
Burnham-on-Crouch 1				51.633041, 0.835061	1914	1919
Burnham-on-Crouch 2	Burnham Wick			51.625571, 0.828763	1934	1939
Burnham-on-Crouch 3		Private strip		51.625769, 0.849219	Unknown	Unknown
Canvey Island					Unknown	Unknown
Chigwell				51.606228, 0.119172	1938	1939
Childerditch		Helipad		51.586561, 0.319147	Unknown	n/a
Chingford				51.634647, -0.023254	1914	1920
Chipping Ongar	Willingale	USAAF	162	51.727567, 0.293992	1943	1948
Clacton				51.784758, 1.130086	1958	n/a
Clacton	Alton Park Road			51.788139, 1.139175	1920s	1939
Clacton		Seaplane			1914	1916
Cocks Clarks	Walton Hall			51.684736, 0.638753	Unknown	2010
Colchester		Hospital		51.910903, 0.899756	Unknown	n/a
Colchester	Merville Barracks	Barracks		51.873818, 0.893726	Unknown	n/a
Dagenham		Helipad		51.512333, 0.161447	Unknown	n/a
Damyns Hall				51.528303, 0.245197	Unknown	n/a
Debden		USAAF	356	51.991469, 0.274278	1937	1975
Docklands	Royal Albert Dock			51.507365, 0.055428	Unknown	Unknown
Downham	Crowsheath Farm				Unknown	Unknown
Earls Colne		USAAF	358	51.910481, 0.685533	1943	n/a
East Hanningfield					Unknown	Unknown
East Horndon					Unknown	Unknown
Easthorpe					Unknown	Unknown
Edneys Common				51.716406, 0.406133	2007	2009

Name 1	Name 2	Notes	AAF Sta.	Lat & Long	Opened	Closed
Fairlop	Hainault Farm			51.592939, 0.099442	1911	1946
Fambridge	South Fambridge			51.631508, 0.681758	1909	1909
Forest Farm				51.600839, 0.101908	Unknown	Unknown
Friday Wood	Colchester				Unknown	Unknown
Fryerning	Hardings Farm			51.686878, 0.377447	Unknown	Unknown
Fyfield				51.741422, 0.279828	1917	1919
Goldhanger	Gardeners Farm			51.739919, 0.740667	1915	1919
Gosfield	Sible Hedingham	USAAF	154	51.950556, 0.583106	Unknown	1953
Great Burstead	Larkins Farm				Unknown	Unknown
Great Dunmow	Little Easton		164	51.884667, 0.310586	1943	1946
Great Oakley				51.912197, 1.182161	2002	n/a
Great Sampford		USAAF	359	51.989317, 0.350803	1942	1948
Great Sampford	Calthorpes Farm	Helipad		52.007108, 0.407711	Unknown	n/a
Great Totham	Scripps Farm			51.778819, 0.694333	Unknown	Unknown
Great Waltham	Fanners Farm			51.782814, 0.430986	Unknown	2010
Great Yeldham				52.014728, 0.554967	Unknown	2014
Hainault Farm				51.600244, 0.118856	1914	1941
Hanningfield	Crowsheath Farm				Unknown	Unknown
Harlow	The Princess Alexandra Hospital	Helipad		51.770914, 0.087814	Unknown	n/a
Harwich					Unknown	Unknown
Herongate	Heron Hall			51.602103, 0.368192	Unknown	2013
High Easter	Easterbury Farm			51.806172, 0.341242	1992	n/a
Hornchurch	Sutton's Farm	RAF		51.537469, 0.211081	1915	1962
Horsey Island				51.876253, 1.231058	Unknown	n/a
Hylands Park	Chelmsford				Unknown	Unknown

Name 1	Name 2	Notes	AAF Sta.	Lat & Long	Opened	Closed
Ingatestone		Second World War, unfinished		51.674478, 0.404003		
Laindon	Bensons Farm			51.593697, 0.444822	Unknown	n/a
Langdon Hills		Winch-launched gliding site			1930	1930
Lippitts Hill		Helipad		51.654389, 0.017642	Unknown	2019
Little Baddow	Retreat Farm			51.746489, 0.595636	Unknown	n/a
Little Burstead	Chase Farm			51.596253, 0.393825	Unknown	n/a
Little Maplestead	Parks Farm			51.982333, 0.669067	Unknown	n/a
Little Totham	Sheepcoates Farm			51.760425, 0.714078	2004	2006
Little Walden	Hadstock	USAAF	165	52.067744, 0.268247	1944	1946
London City	Docklands			51.504914, 0.056003	1987	n/a
Maplin Sands					Unknown	Unknown
Margaretting					Unknown	Unknown
Matching	Matching Green	USAAF	166	51.782219, 0.241283	1943	1946
Maylands	Romford			51.607472, 0.253748	1928	1939
Mountnessing					1916	1916
Navestock	Jenkins Farm			51.640558, 0.202861	Unknown	n/a
North Benfleet				51.564619, 0.538589	1916	1919
North Weald	North Weald Bassett	RAF		51.718933, 0.153056	1916	n/a
Norwood Lodge					2007	n/a
Orsett				51.501153, 0.389889	1916	1919
Palmers Farm	Shenfield			51.650805, 0.315605	1917	1919
Plough Corner	Little Clacton			51.838372, 1.139531	1916	1919
Rayne	Rayne Hall Farm			51.885394, 0.521964	1996	n/a
Ridgewell		USAAF	167	52.044633, 0.559100	1942	1957
Rivenhall	Silver End	USAAF	168	51.855011, 0.641708	1943	1946
Runwell	Wickford			51.626546, 0.523771	1917	1919

Name 1	Name 2	Notes	AAF Sta.	Lat & Long	Opened	Closed
Sewards Hall Farm					Unknown	Unknown
Sible Hedingham	Blooms Farm			51.994428, 0.555381	Unknown	n/a
Sladbury's Farm					1992	Unknown
Southend	Rochford	International airport		51.572264, 0.698456	1915	Unknown
Southminster	West Newlands Farm				Unknown	Unknown
Springfield	Pump Lane				Unknown	Unknown
Springfield	Sandford Road				Unknown	Unknown
St Lawrence	Newlands Farm			51.690028, 0.820581	Unknown	n/a
St Osyth	Lodge Farm			51.796503, 1.105406	Unknown	n/a
Stansted	Stansted Mountfitchet	International airport	169	51.885747, 0.236628	1943	n/a
Stapleford Tawney	Stapleford	RAF		51.652811, 0.155983	1934	n/a
Steeple Bumpstead	Wildings Farm			52.030078, 0.448861	Unknown	n/a
Stock	Brocks Farm			51.656197, 0.420881	Unknown	n/a
Stow Maries	Flambirds			51.669736, 0.632403	1916	1919
Takeley		Helipad		51.869419, 0.247869	Unknown	n/a
Thaxted				51.963727, 0.368685	1916	1919
Thorpe-le-Soken	Green Farm			51.865842, 1.143992	1986	2007
Thurrock				51.537411, 0.367092	1984	n/a
Tillingham	Stowes Farm			51.693033, 0.872867	1984	n/a
Upminster	Gerpins Farm			51.531492, 0.231542	Unknown	n/a
Weeley Heath	Lodge Farm				Unknown	Unknown
West Bergholt	Manor Farm			51.918139, 0.860600	Unknown	n/a
West Horndon	Barnards Farm			51.563972, 0.355258	Unknown	n/a
Wethersfield	Ostlers Farm			51.964464, 0.513792	Unknown	n/a
Wethersfield		USAAF	170	51.971236, 0.509817	1944	1990
Wethersfield	Whitehall Farm			51.968233, 0.522508	Unknown	n/a

Name 1	Name 2	Notes	AAF Sta.	Lat & Long	Opened	Closed
Wickford	Elm Farm			51.608686, 0.481583	Unknown	2008
Wickham St Paul	Stones Farm			51.988958, 0.657597	Unknown	n/a
Widford	Chelmsford			51.723539, 0.446321	1914	1915
Woodham Mortimer	Lodge Farm			51.721917, 0.627992	Unknown	2017
Wormingford		USAAF	159	51.940036, 0.792106	1917	1947
Writtle	Chelmsford			51.733273, 0.432129	1914	1916

A brick-built memorial unveiled in 2014 to remember the twenty-three American servicemen and one British civilian killed in the explosion of a B-17 Flying Fortress at Ridgewell on 23 June 1943. (Paul Bingley)